Uncover Norway's Intriguing Origins: The Ultimate Research Companion

Sameer .P Haley

All rights reserved. Copyright © 2023 Sameer .P Haley

Funny helpful tips:

In the garden of life, nurture the seeds of kindness, love, and compassion.

Incorporate a balanced intake of macronutrients; proteins, fats, and carbohydrates all play essential roles in health and fitness.

Uncover Norway's Intriguing Origins: The Ultimate Research Companion : Unlock the Enigmatic Past of Norway: Your Essential Guide to Thorough Research on Norwegian Origins.

Life advices:

Nurture trust; it's the foundation of a secure relationship.

Engage with the world of smart contracts; they automate and verify contractual processes on blockchain platforms.

Introduction

This book unfolds the rich tapestry of Scandinavia, weaving together the threads of its prehistoric roots, warrior societies, Viking Age glory, and the intricate political dance that shaped the nation. Journey through time as we explore the foundations and evolution of Norway, from its early inhabitants to the aftermath of World War II.

The tale begins in prehistory, where the rugged landscapes of Scandinavia were witness to the emergence of its first inhabitants. From hunters to the pioneers of agriculture, the early chapters of Norway's history reveal the resilience and adaptability of its people. The Bronze Age introduces us to a warrior society, leaving behind settlements that echo tales of a bygone era.

The Iron Age unfolds with tales of warfare and the emergence of the Sámi people, shaping the cultural landscape of northern Norway. The Viking Age, a period synonymous with Norse prowess, is spotlighted with its exploration, trade, and the unification of Norway under powerful leaders.

As Christianity spreads, Norway's medieval history is marked by the church's influence, aristocracy, and societal dynamics. The Black Death casts its shadow, altering the socio-economic landscape and leading Norway toward the Scandinavian Union. The narrative delves into the Denmark-Norway period, navigating through constitutional politics and the complexities of union with Sweden.

The early modern period brings economic shifts and constitutional developments, setting the stage for an independent Norway within the Union with Sweden. The 19th century sees the birth of a new state, marked by recovery, growth, and political changes.

The 20th century catapults Norway into the global arena, with neutrality during World War II, resistance against occupation, and the nation's remarkable recovery afterward. The narrative concludes with the post-war era, where Norway emerges as a sovereign nation, embracing modernity while cherishing its historical roots.

This book is not just a chronological account; it's an exploration of the forces that shaped the identity of a nation. Join us on this captivating journey through Norway's past, where each chapter unfolds like a well-preserved artifact, revealing the resilience, aspirations, and indomitable spirit of a remarkable people.

Contents

Chapter 1 – Scandinavia in Prehistory 1
    The Founders of Scandinavia 5
    The Hunters 8
    The First Farmers 10

Chapter 2 – Bronze and Iron Age Warriors 14
    The Bronze Age (1700–500 BCE) 14
    The Warrior Society of the Bronze Age 16
    Bronze Age Settlements 18
    The Iron Age (500 BCE–750 CE) 20
    Iron Age Warfare 23
    The Iron Age in the North and the Sámi People 25

Chapter 3 – The Viking Age in Norway 29
    The Viking Age in Norway 32
    The Unification of Norway 36
    Old Religion and the Spread of Christianity 41

Chapter 4 – Norway in the Middle Ages 45
    The Medieval Church, Aristocracy, and Wide Society 46
    The Black Death and the Hanseatic League 50
    Toward the Scandinavian Union 53

Chapter 5 – Denmark-Norway, 1536–1814 56
    The Early Modern Period 58
    The Economy 63
    Land Ownership 65
    Constitutional Politics 67

    The Norwegian Outlook on the Union 69
Chapter 6 – The Union with Sweden 72
    The Relationship of Denmark-Norway and Sweden 73
    The Crisis Years 75
    Independence in the Union with Sweden 77
    The Constitution 79
Chapter 7 – The New State 81
    Recovery and Growth of Norway 83
    The Embedsmann State 86
    The Beginning of Modern Norway 88
    Political Changes 89
    Norway Stays Neutral 92
Chapter 8 – World War II 98
    Norway Becomes an Ally 100
    The Country and Society under the Occupation 102
    Norway's Resistance Movement 104
    After the War 105
Conclusion 108

Chapter 1 – Scandinavia in Prehistory

Satellite image of Scandinavia from March 2002.

https://commons.wikimedia.org/wiki/File:Scandinavia_M2002074_lrg.jpg

To understand the history of Norway, you must understand its geographical position and the history of the whole of Scandinavia. Scandinavia is not strictly a geographical term. It is used to designate culturally, linguistically, and historically similar countries: Denmark, Sweden, and Norway. In a geographical sense, Scandinavia is a peninsula, and as such, it includes mainland Norway, Sweden, and parts of Finland and Russia. But in a cultural sense, Scandinavia is often expanded to include the Faroe Islands, Iceland, the Åland Islands, Svalbard, and Greenland. Norway is part of this cultural and geographical region, and its early history is very connected to its neighboring countries. This is why when researching the earliest history of Norway, the best thing to do is look at the history of the whole of Scandinavia, both in the geographical and cultural sense.

The prehistory of Scandinavia started more than thirteen thousand years ago at the very end of the last glacial period. Global warming started, the ice melted, and new lands for flora and fauna to thrive opened up. The first humans then came to live in the Scandinavian region and started their Stone Age culture. In Scandinavia, the Stone Age is divided into three phases: Old or Hunter Stone Age (Paleolithic period), Middle Stone Age (Mesolithic), and New or Farmer Stone Age (Neolithic period). The Stone Age in Scandinavia lasted from 13,000 to 1700 BCE. The Bronze Age lasted between 1700 and 500 BCE. The next was the Iron Age, which lasted from 500 BCE until the start of the Viking Age, approximately 750 CE. However, although this periodization is largely accepted for the whole of Scandinavia, it cannot be applied to the northern regions. There, the climate was such that development was often halted, and some changes didn't appear at all. For example, the true Neolithic period never really arrived in the north since agriculture was impossible due to permafrost.

The first societies of Scandinavia, those belonging to the early Paleolithic, are almost invisible to archaeologists and history in general. They were hunters, and they inhabited mainly the western shores of the peninsula, where they had easy access to reindeer and seals. Their tools were made of stone, animal bones, and antlers, and they were scattered across the landscape. It is hard for scholars to determine what kind of social structure these early societies had, if they even had any. But with the Neolithic period came the first permanent settlements on the western shores, although they were very small. Several huts and burial places belonging to this period were discovered, as well as flint items, seashells, and fish bones, which points to a culture capable of utilizing resources from the sea. The first pottery appeared in the late Mesolithic period, but it became much more common in the Neolithic.

In the Neolithic period, the societies of Scandinavia turned to farming. The first farms were established in inland Scandinavia, where the land was more fertile. Pastures for cattle were also more available there. This is also the period where the people started burying their dead in monumental tombs, which held tens, sometimes even hundreds of bodies. During the early Neolithic period, copper items appeared, and they became common later in this period. Although some houses and many tombs from the Neolithic period were preserved, especially in southern Scandinavia, not much is known about the society. However, with the start of the Bronze Age, this changed.

The Bronze Age is best known for the usage of this metal, but it was also the first appearance of social structures. The tribes were led by chiefs, who resided in large timber halls, and were buried with their riches and weapons, many of which had their origins in other parts of Europe. The rest of the people were simple farmers living on scattered small farmsteads. The commoners were still buried together, but some prominent individuals and even whole families had special, designated burial spaces within the common burial complex. This whole period was dominated by rich individuals, and most of the archaeological and historical evidence belongs to the chieftains. The rest of Scandinavian society remains almost invisible to history.

During the Iron Age, true villages emerged. Many large and small farms have been excavated, and flint and stone completely perished as a material used for tools and weapons. With the villages came more powerful leaders who were capable of directing the economic and social developments of their people. Military and religious activities became apparent, and the chieftains often assumed the roles of military and religious leaders. Society was divided into distinct classes, such as warriors, shamans (or priests), artists, and craftsmen. The people of the Iron Age started changing the landscape of Scandinavia as they built roads and bridges, erected walls around their settlements, and built fortresses. The burial mounds became larger so they could accommodate more people, more treasures of the chieftains, and sometimes even whole ships.

The Founders of Scandinavia

Human ancestors first arrived in Europe more than a million years ago. But they were mostly concentrated in the south and southwestern regions of the continent, as the climate there allowed them to thrive. They were hunter-gatherers, and they led a nomadic way of life. They were constantly on the move and in search of food sources. When the ice melted in the north of Europe, it left behind a wide territory covered in tall grass and thick wild birch forests. These were the perfect conditions for the migration of animals. While the birch forests became home to large elk, the grasslands and plains of the northern tundra attracted reindeer. For a very long time, it was believed that the first Scandinavians came from southwestern Europe as they followed the migration of large elk, and although this is true, they were not the only ones. At approximately the same time, another group of people migrated to the western shores of

Scandinavia, and they came from the east. They were the nomadic people of northern Russia, and they came to the far west of Norway by traversing the arctic routes of Russia, Finland, and Sweden, all while following the migration of reindeer.

The earliest known Scandinavian body ever discovered is Koelbjerg Man, and it was discovered in Denmark. His remains were carbon-dated to around 8000 BCE. Later, the remains of a settlement were found approximately two kilometers south from the site where Koelbjerg Man was found. This settlement was also dated to the year 8000 BCE, and it is quite possible the man lived there. However, these discoveries are not the oldest ones in Scandinavia. In the north of Norway, the first archaeological findings were dated to 9000 BCE, and they were tools and items belonging to the people who came from the east and settled on the western shores of Scandinavia. It is believed that these people then constructed crude vessels made of animal skins and sailed to the south, where they eventually met the migrating southwestern Europeans.

It is from the mingling of the southwestern and northeastern migratory nomadic tribes that the first cultures developed in Scandinavia. The two most prominent ones in Norway were the Hensbacka and Fosna cultures. A third one was discovered in the Alta region in northern Norway and was named the Komsa culture after Mount Komsa. However, most recent discoveries proved that the Komsa culture was, in fact, the same as Fosna, but due to the lack of flint and some other materials in the northernmost reaches of Norway, the Komsa culture lacked diversity in their tools. The Hensbacka culture was mainly concentrated on the shores of western Sweden and the Oslofjord in Norway, while Fosna/Komsa spread from the central (Trøndelag county) to northern Norway (Finnmark). Even though archaeologically these two cultures were different, they are generally called the Fosna-Hensbacka culture due to their undeniable similarities.

The Fosna-Hensbacka culture is typically dated between 9000 and 8000 BCE, and the tools belonging to it are usually large flake axes and artifacts with distinctive tanged points. The design of the flake axes suggests they were used as an adze instead of an ax, as the blade was perpendicular to the shaft. They were also very similar to the *ulu* of the Inuits, a long crescent-shaped blade used for butchering seals and food preparation. Flint was the main material from which the tools of the Fosna-Hensbacka culture were made, but Scandinavia had very few sources of flint. The earliest source came from Denmark and southwestern Sweden. It is believed that flint was taken from these parts and traded elsewhere either as already prepared tools or as a raw material. Later, flint sources were found along the southwestern beaches of Norway, and it is believed that the early people used icebergs to transport flint to the northern areas. In other areas of Scandinavia where flint was sparse or didn't exist, the people used other materials to construct their tools, such as chert, rhyolite, tuff, jasper, rock crystal, and fine-grained quartzite.

For a long time, it was believed that the north of Norway and Scandinavia in general were populated much later than the south. For this reason, the history of northern Scandinavia was often neglected, and no archaeological excavations were performed. However, once archaeological findings were discovered, scholars were shocked to learn that the northernmost reaches of the peninsula were inhabited at the same time as the south. All the items found in the early northern settlements were as old as those found in the southern settlements. But their similarity with the southern inhabitants came as the result of the mixing between the early migratory peoples.

Just as in the south, the northern society was sea-oriented. The eastern parts of the Scandinavian Peninsula were still covered in ice, and glaciers dominated the area. But the shore was habitable, and the sea was filled with life. Most of the settlements above the Arctic Circle were concentrated on the western shores of Norway and the coast of the Russian Kola Peninsula. The materials most often used here were various quartzites, cherts, and flint of very poor quality. But it is there, in the far north, that the earliest rock art was discovered. In the Nordland region, at the end of the Komsa period, the people started carving shapes of animals into the surrounding rocks. These animals were usually whales, reindeer, elk, and bears, and they were dated to 8000 BCE.

The Hunters

Scandinavia is a vast territory, and as such, it has different conditions for life in the southern and northern areas. The Old Stone Age, also known as the Hunter Stone Age because this was the period when hunter-gatherer societies thrived, lasted approximately from 9700 BCE until 4000 BCE. However, in the far north, where the land couldn't be cultivated due to climate and permafrost, the hunter-gatherer societies existed much longer than in the south; some even exist today. But these societies left very little behind, and we know almost nothing about how they lived and what their social structure was like.

Their main tools were adapted to hunting, and various arrowheads and spearheads have been found that tell the story of their development. At the beginning of the Stone Age, arrowheads were narrow and long. While they would easily reach their target, they would slice through animal tissue, causing little damage. As time passed, the northerners adapted their weapons and started producing wider arrowheads that would smash bone tissue and cause much more damage to the animal, which made hunting more efficient.

At the end of the Stone Age, pottery was introduced to Scandinavia. More and more jars and different varieties of pottery containers can be found in the Mesolithic archaeological sites that were dated after 4800 BCE. It was believed that pottery was introduced to Scandinavia from southern Europe. However, recent discoveries proved that Scandinavian pottery came from the east, following the northern routes from China through Russia and Finland. There might have been more than one source from which Scandinavian pottery originated, but the prevailing opinion is that it was introduced from the east. In southern Scandinavia, where the climate was milder, other materials were used for producing tools and ornamental objects, such as bones, antlers, amber, wood, tree bark, and fungus threads.

The climate during the Scandinavian Stone Age was warming up, and thick forests of birch, pine, and hazel developed in places that previously belonged to the tundra. Over time, as the warming up continued, elm, oak, and lime trees started appearing. The different types of trees and forests attracted different types of animals, which people could hunt. Red deer, wild pig, and roe deer became the most valued prey, and they drove the economy of the hunter-gatherer societies of the north. Marten, otter, wildcat, and squirrel were other animals hunted for their fur and meat. The Hunter Stone Age is also the period in which the first dogs started appearing in the tombs of humans, a clear sign of domestication. Thus, dogs were the first animals to be domesticated, even before the development of agriculture. Although it is unknown where and when the first dogs joined humans, one theory suggests it happened in northern Siberia. After the last glacial period, most of the Scandinavians lived by the sea, and the warming climate made the waters abundant with life. The main diet of the Scandinavian hunter-gatherers came from the sea in the form of fish, crustaceans, mollusks, seals, and even whales. Freshwater fish was also popular among the early Scandinavian societies, as the melting glaciers formed a great number of lakes and rivers. The equipment they used to extract fish and sea mammals was very elaborate. They used rods, hooks, spears, and even nets made out of bark and fungus threads. Because most archaeological sites contained a very large number of animal bones and antlers, it was believed that land mammals were the main diet of the Stone Age hunter-gatherers. However, the carbon isotope ratios in human bones from the Mesolithic period correspond to those of the Greenlandic Inuit, whose diet primarily consisted of marine sources. The human remains of the Neolithic period when farming was introduced have a carbon isotope ratio appropriate for a diet based on plants and domestic land animals. Today, it is believed that the Scandinavian hunter-gatherers had 75 percent of their diet coming from the sea. The shift in diet was very sharp once farming was introduced to southern Scandinavia.

What little is known about these early Scandinavian societies seems to be much different than what is generally believed about the European hunter-gatherers. While in central Europe, these societies were very small and constantly on the move in search of prey, in Scandinavia, they were much larger, and they preferred to stay in one region. This might be because the density of people in central Europe was very small during the Stone Age, and in the north, people concentrated around the seashores where the climate was warmer and food resources abundant. But that doesn't mean that all societies in the Scandinavian Stone Age were sedentary. Some people followed large land animals, mainly reindeer, as they migrated to the colder north, although their numbers were very small since the majority preferred to stay near the sea.

The First Farmers

The most important event in human prehistory is the transition from hunting and gathering to farming. This shift from foraging for food to producing it changed the way of living for humans across the globe, and it was no different in Scandinavia. This is why scholars are very interested in finding out and explaining what pushed the people to make such a change and how this transition influenced all aspects

of life. Scientists started researching this topic in the early 19th century, and even Charles Darwin engaged in the research of the domestication of plants and animals. In Scandinavia, agriculture began with the appearance of the Funnelbeaker culture (named so because of the shape of the ceramics found in the archaeological sites).

The Funnelbeaker culture appeared first around 5000 BCE in what is today northern Germany, but it reached Scandinavia only one thousand years later. Once it arrived, the life of the people abruptly changed. Scholars are still researching what exactly caused this sudden change. Domesticated animals and plants appeared as if out of nowhere, and it took only a few hundreds of years for the whole Scandinavian society to change its way of life. But this wasn't the case only in northern Europe. Wherever agriculture appeared, change came surprisingly fast. The first items signaling the arrival of agriculture were the T-shaped axes made out of copper and jadeite, as well as some copper ornamental items, such as rings and bracelets. These were imported into Scandinavia directly from Germany and Poland, but the domestication of animals and plants had yet to come.

There is not a lot of evidence for farming during the first part of the Neolithic period. Several settlements were discovered, and there are only a few signs of purposeful deforestation, which would have opened the fields for agriculture. But around 3500 BCE, the development of agriculture exploded. But it is yet to be discovered how farming first arrived in Scandinavia. Three main theories could explain the appearance of farming in northern Europe: 1) the colonization of the Scandinavian Peninsula by the southern Europeans, 2) the adoption of agriculture by the indigenous people, 3) or the combination of the two elements, with small groups of new settlers bringing the idea of agriculture, which was then quickly adopted by the indigenous people.

The contact between the Danubian farming societies and the southern Scandinavians existed even in the late Mesolithic and early Neolithic periods, which can be seen from the import of tools and jewelry. But it is suspected that the idea of agriculture didn't get adopted early simply because the sea-oriented Scandinavians didn't have much use for it. The waters were abundant with food, and coastal life was thriving. So, the reason they suddenly changed from hunting and fishing to agriculture remains a mystery. Perhaps it was the increase in population or the decline of available resources that made the people turn to growing their own food. Some scholars even propose that it wasn't any natural cause that caused the transition to farming but a socio-economic change. The hunter-gatherer societies started forming classes, and the elites needed to create a surplus in food to keep their social position. This could only be achieved through farming.

The first plants that were grown in Neolithic Scandinavia were emmer, einkorn, naked barley, wheat, and probably spelt. Oil-rich plants were also domesticated early, as well as some berries, apples, and nuts. Aside from plants, the Neolithic Scandinavians domesticated animals, such as pigs, cattle, sheep, goats, and dogs. As discussed earlier, dogs were the first animals to appear alongside humans. The other animals didn't appear in Scandinavia until approximately 3800 BCE. During the Funnelbeaker culture in Scandinavia, around 90 percent of animal bones found in archaeological sites belonged to domesticated animals.

It seems that cattle were the most prominent animal. They were highly regarded for their meat and milk, which could be consumed, and also because of their skin, horns, and bones, which were used for tool production. Cattle were so widespread that they came to represent 80 percent of domestic animals in later Neolithic sites. Pigs were also popular, but they were mostly kept in the settlements away from the sea where they could roam the forests. Sheep and goats were also present but not as widespread as cattle and pigs. It is therefore unlikely that wool was used for textile production at this period and that the main material for garments was probably leather and fur.

With agriculture came a wide change in the society of Scandinavia, and different cultures started developing. Some focused on their warrior lifestyle, while others started practicing nomadic cattle herding. Some were completely sedentary societies that developed early forms of village life, while others chose to move around, following animal migrations or simply conquering their weaker neighbors. But the prevailing culture of the late Neolithic period was the Bell Beaker culture (named after the pottery shape they used the most). It seems they were mostly traders in northern and central Europe. They produced and exchanged flint daggers, spears, and tools, and they introduced the first metals to Scandinavia. The southern people had already discovered metals, especially copper, gold, and later bronze, and they used them in trading. Following the economic network of late Neolithic Scandinavia and Europe in general, these metals found their way to the north.

The introduction of metals, just like agriculture, started a new series of changes within Scandinavian society. Mainly, the society started dividing itself by class, and powerful warrior chieftains became the leaders of small or large groups of people. Due to this power, they were able to conquer their neighbors and establish long-distance trade routes that would bring them even more riches. But all these changes mainly occurred in the southern regions of Scandinavia, where agriculture bloomed. Northern Norway and Sweden felt the influences from the south, and they started using newly developed and imported tools and materials, but agriculture was still impossible there. This is why the social changes were almost nonexistent in northern Scandinavia. Nevertheless, the Bronze Age arrived in Scandinavia, and it would become one of the most remarkable periods of Scandinavian prehistory.

Chapter 2 – Bronze and Iron Age Warriors

Reconstructed longhouse at the archaeological site at Borg, modern Viking Museum.
I, Jörg Hempel, CC BY-SA 2.0 DE https://creativecommons.org/licenses/by-sa/2.0/de/deed.en via Wikimedia Commons
https://commons.wikimedia.org/wiki/File:Borg_Vestv%C3%A5g%C3%B8y_LC0165.jpg

The Bronze Age (1700–500 BCE)

The European Bronze Age originated in the Aegean area, where it started around 3000 BCE. But it came late to Scandinavia, just as agriculture did. The Scandinavian Bronze Age started in 1700 BCE and lasted until 500 BCE, and it was followed by the Iron Age. However, bronze items were already in use in Scandinavia before the proper Bronze Age came. This is because of the extensive trade network the Scandinavians developed with the rest of Europe, especially with areas that are today central Germany and Poland.

From there, copper and bronze items, such as tools and jewelry, entered the north, although Scandinavians didn't start producing their own metal items yet. The Bronze Age is not only about the use of metal; it also brought social and economic changes. Although the metal was in use in Scandinavia as early as 2800 BCE, the social changes didn't occur until 1600 BCE.

Although the Bronze Age started late in Scandinavia, it was a very productive period, as there are more bronze artifacts found in this peninsula than anywhere else in Europe. However, flint continued to be used for the production of daggers and scraping tools. Metal items used in Scandinavia were mostly imported. It was only during the Late Bronze Age that production started. However, once it was set in motion, metal production became the basis of the Scandinavian economy. Almost all of the production sites were concentrated in the southern parts of the peninsula, but ingots were imported. Middle Sweden and southern Norway have rich copper veins, but these were not excavated during the Bronze Age. Nevertheless, the items produced from imported ore and ingots were usually for local use and often found in the burial mounds. The most common bronze items produced in Scandinavia were richly decorated shields and lures (also spelled as lurs; they are very long horns used to make music).

Most of the raw ores for the production of bronze items were imported from the western Mediterranean world, and it is believed that the Scandinavians sailed the Atlantic routes for trade. But the style of the items produced in Scandinavia wasn't Mediterranean-styled. Instead, they preferred central European aesthetics and were influenced by the items they saw in central Germany, Poland, and even Latvia. With the new metals and stylistic designs came new ideas, and these were also borrowed mostly from central Europe. By the second millennium BCE, northern Europe started producing a great number of innovative items, such as chariots and new weapons. But the most intriguing change came within the society, as the first social institutions were created. Agriculture was no longer the only viable foundation for the economy. Now trade, crafts, and production entered the scene and started competing with farming.

The new economic foundations brought an even greater accumulation of wealth and power, and competition became fierce. This led to an increased number of conflicts and open wars between different groups of people. The result was a constant change in trade alliances, the creation of new ones, and old trade ties being cut off. The differences in the social status of individuals became very prominent, and the idea of land ownership was introduced into Scandinavian society. Wealthy individuals were able to afford extra workers in their chosen industries, and captured enemies became slaves. The differences in social status are observable today, as the burial mounds from the Bronze Age were well preserved. These mounds often contain enormous riches, such as weapons, clothes, household items, chariots, and animals. The chieftains and high-status individuals were buried in stone and wood coffins, while the commoners were buried without any protective layer around them. The Late Bronze Age saw the widespread use of cremation, and although it often signaled the equal treatment of the dead in the afterlife, in Scandinavia, the ashes of prominent individuals were buried with their riches to put an accent on their high status during life.

The Warrior Society of the Bronze Age

The Bronze Age excavations led to extraordinary discoveries in Scandinavia. One was the existence of a new social class: the warriors. Separate graves were found in which warriors were buried with special honors. They were different from the graves of the chieftains and commoners, as the items they contained pointed to a lifestyle of continuous warfare. These individuals were always buried with their armor and weapons. The main items found in these tombs were swords, shields, and items for personal hygiene, such as combs, trimmers, and mirrors. The Early Bronze Age saw the redesign of arrows and spears, as these were weapons adapted from hunting. However, when swords and battle-axes came into use, their number significantly decreased.

The sword was the first weapon specifically designed for battle, and they were meant for close hand-to-hand combat. Bronze weapons were also used as a symbol of high social status, as they must have been expensive to produce. Copies of these bronze swords were also produced out of flint so they could be used by less fortunate individuals. All bronze and flint swords excavated in Scandinavia that date to the Bronze Age display signs of frequent usage. They were often sharpened and contained many nicks, though these were often removed before burial. Swords that were placed as offerings were never repaired and sharpened. In Scandinavia, two types of swords were in use: ones with a solid metal hilt riveted to the blade and those that had the blade and the hilt cast together.

Although warriors represented a new social class that rose in response to the increased need for the defense of communities, their bodies rarely displayed signs of violent death. But this could be due to the poor skeletal preservation of the Early Bronze Age. During the Late Bronze Age, the bodies were cremated, and there is no way of concluding how they died. Nevertheless, scholars estimate that the life expectancy in Scandinavia during the Bronze Age was around forty years.

One archaeological site in Norway, near the city of Trondheim, serves as evidence that violent deaths did occur. This place named Sund is actually a part of a wider excavation area that extends to another dig site named Tunds. It seems that the people of these two sites were two parts of the same society. Sund proved to be a mass grave, where the bones of humans were mixed with those of animals. The human bones belonged to men, women, and children. Around 50 percent of the discovered remains belonged to children. They were dated to approximately the same period as the remains found two kilometers to the west in Tunds.

But there was a massive difference between these two sites. The burials in Tunds were done appropriately for the period, and many personal items, weapons, and armor were found together with human remains, which were buried separate from each other. In Sund, all remains were found together in one massive grave, and they had no personal items with them. Further exploration of the remains proved that the ones found in Tunds belonged to healthy individuals, all aged above forty. Those found in Sund displayed various signs of malnutrition and bone defects that are common for hard-working people (spondylosis and osteoarthritis). Bone cuts could often be seen on the remains of the adult individuals from Sund but not on the children. Some of these cuts healed, but some were made immediately before death and had no time to heal. The bone cuts are a perfect sign of the violence these people must have experienced.

Scholars believed that the inhabitants of Sund were warriors due to the signs of violence their remains showed and the lack of these signs on the remains of the children. However, the deformities of the bones caused by malnutrition and hard work are not found among any other remains of warrior societies around the world. Therefore, it must have been that the Sund people were oppressed, probably by their very close neighbors of Tunds. In fact, there is a high possibility that Sund and Tunds were the same community, with the first one being the slums in which the slaves lived and the latter being home to a warrior society. This would explain the malnutrition and bone deformities and wounds, as well as the fact that they were all buried in a single grave. The Sund inhabitants possibly died all at approximately the same time, either due to violence or disease.

Bronze Age Settlements

The typical form of settlements in the Scandinavian Bronze Age were farmsteads. They were rarely fenced, and they were close to each other. A group of such farmsteads formed a community, and the chieftain had the largest land allotment and the largest house, which was typically in the middle of the settlement. Farmhouses were more simple and smaller than the houses of the Late Neolithic period, probably because of the lack of wood for construction. The forests were cut down long before to make room for farms n. Typically, the longhouse belonged to the chieftain, and it served as a hall. However, it also housed the extended family of the Bronze Age leaders. Some houses in southern Sweden had a separate room with a hearth that housed a family and another one for the animals. However, sheltering the animals wasn't practiced anywhere else in Scandinavia until the Iron Age.

Some of the houses had cellars in which food was stored, but these were rare. The houses were built on or near the site of an old house that was deteriorated. Repairing houses wasn't profitable, and the Bronze Age people preferred to build a new one once the old house was no longer usable. Nevertheless, the settlements were very stable, and they remained inhabited for long periods. Families often buried their dead on their farmsteads, which took up several square kilometers. The distance between farmsteads indicates that the settlements weren't yet proper villages. The typical layout of the settlement was one large farmstead, which belonged to a chieftain, that was surrounded by many smaller farms.

The Bronze Age settlement development in the north of Scandinavia was very much different than in the south. There, farming finally arrived, but due to the climate, it could only be practiced in the coastal regions. The tools used by these northern farmers remained largely made out of stone, as metal hadn't yet entered this region. Nevertheless, farming spread north of Trondheim to the Altafjord in Norway, and the people learned how to grow their food. Hunter-gatherers still thrived, though. The seas were still rich in fish, and although plant-based food could be cultivated, the Bronze Age north Scandinavians continued to hunt and fish. Hunter-gatherer societies continued to exist in inland areas and the far north, but they formed new alliances and trade connections with the southerners. In exchange for new tools and weapons, they traded meat and fur.

The Bronze Age might have been the period when the Sámi people first appeared in Scandinavia. However, it is impossible to conclude how long they roamed the peninsula due to their constant nomadic way of life, which they have managed to preserve even today. Nevertheless, the connection of the Scandinavians with the Russians, Finnish, and Eastern Baltics increased during the Bronze Age, especially in the north. The eastern ideas continued to flow into Scandinavia, and they can be easily seen in clothing decorations, asbestos-tempered ceramics, and elongated stone projectiles. In the north of Norway and Sweden, distinctive rock carvings with elaborate drawings of animals, people, boats, and abstract objects and shapes have been discovered that can be connected to the shamanistic religion of the period. These carvings and drawings can be found in northern Norway, Sweden, Finland, and the Russian Kola Peninsula. The wide area in which they are found might be explained by the nomadic way of life of the northernmost societies.

The Iron Age (500 BCE–750 CE)

The Scandinavian Iron Age came later than in the rest of Europe, and it is divided into three periods: pre-Roman, Roman, and Germanic. The names of this division can be confusing since the Romans never conquered Scandinavia, and they barely even knew about these northern regions. Nevertheless, the Roman influence on the whole of Europe was so great that it was felt even in the far north. The Iron Age was followed by the Viking period, which some scholars see as the peak of the Scandinavian Iron Age, as it happened just before the beginning of the medieval period and the spread of Christianity in the north. But even though the Viking period can be considered part of the Iron Age, more about it will be said in the next chapter.

The Romans never sent their legions to Scandinavia, and they never spread their military influence to the peninsula. In fact, they never went east of the Rhine River, and their politics never concerned the northern people. So, how did they manage to spread their influence without stepping on Scandinavian soil? The Roman Empire was one of the largest empires in the world, and it was the most significant empire in the history of Europe. As such, it had an extremely vast economic network that spread as far as China in the east and to the westernmost coast of Europe. This economic network also included Scandinavia. Roman goods and commodities moved across Asia and Europe, and some of them would reach Scandinavia. The northerners traded raw materials and slaves to acquire Roman glass, pottery, weapons, and various exotic metal objects that came from all corners of Europe and even Asia.

Although the Scandinavians never extracted metal during the Bronze Age, after 500 BCE, they started excavating iron from local deposits. They sold it as a raw material, but the Scandinavians also developed iron products. The newly discovered material was stronger than bronze; therefore, it was more suitable for the production of weapons and farming tools. The excavation of iron in northern Europe was much different than in the rest of the continent. Iron was typically mined from the mountains, such as the Carpathians, the Alps, or the Holy Cross Mountains in modern-day Poland. But in the lowlands of southern Scandinavia, iron could be found by forming a thin layer in the boggy ground.

Because of this, the Scandinavians couldn't simply adopt the excavation methods from other Europeans. Instead, they had to look to western Asia and adapt their own method of iron extraction. They had to collect the bog iron sand and use sophisticated furnaces and technology to melt and separate iron. The production of iron was very expensive because it demanded time, plenty of raw materials, and a labor force that would mind the furnaces for hours. To make just one kilogram (2.2 pounds) of iron, a furnace needed to work continuously for 25 hours and consume 10 kilograms (22 pounds) of charcoal. Only wealthy individuals were able to start iron production in Scandinavia.

The settlements of the pre-Roman Iron Age remained the same as during the Bronze Age, but the size of the farmhouses started varying more. This is a good indicator of the divisions of society, which became much wider with the introduction of the new metal and new economy. Certain individuals were rich and able to build larger farms and houses, while the rest had to be satisfied with smaller ones. During the Roman Iron Age, the farms gained true fences. Suddenly, people started reinforcing their position against their neighbors. This meant that the relationships within a community changed. Although the main unit of a settlement remained a farm, the communities slowly started taking the shape of true villages.

The settlements in eastern and central Scandinavia were suddenly abandoned during the 6th century CE, even those that were permanently inhabited for over a thousand years. Between 536 and 545, a climatic catastrophe occurred in Eurasia, but modern scholars are unsure what exactly happened. The mainstream opinion is that it was a combination of several volcanic eruptions and a meteorite crash. The written accounts from Europe of the period talk about the sun barely showing, as if a veil of dust had enveloped the earth. The summer temperatures dropped by 4°C (7°F), and the sky was always darkened. Thus, the plants couldn't grow.

This natural catastrophe was so great that even Mesopotamia recorded frost and snow during the summer of 536. In Scandinavia, this period saw an increase of sacrificial items, which suggests that people tried to fend off the natural catastrophe with religious rituals. Some scholars even believe that this period was a source of inspiration for the myth of *Fimbulwinter* ("Great Winter," which lasted for three years without a summer), a prelude to Ragnarök, the end of the known world and the birth of a new one.

But the abandonment of the settlements wasn't uncommon in the Iron Age. As farmers exhausted the land that they grew food on, whole communities would move to a new area with more fertile land. This movement caused the development of different types of settlements during the Late Iron Age. Some remained small, but there is no doubt the size of settlements continuously grew and that communities often merged to form larger villages. The community leaders also grew more powerful, and their titles became hereditary. Local chieftains turned into true rulers, resembling medieval kingship. These powerful rulers had the means to extend their trade network beyond the Rhine and Germany into the Roman Empire. They even started several important economic centers in Scandinavia, such as Uppåkra, Gudme, Sorte Muld, and Gamla Uppsala.

Iron Age Warfare

The culture of Iron Age Scandinavia was even more warrior-oriented than the one of the Bronze Age. The first iron items produced were weapons, and they were used to defend and conquer new lands or people. Warfare was the norm throughout Europe during the Iron Age, and it was no different in Scandinavia. The territories were divided, militarized, and fortified. The excavated bodies that belong to the Iron Age display clear signs of violent deaths, and more male bodies were buried with weapons and armor. This pattern of warfare, which started in the Late Bronze Age and culminated during the Iron Age, would remain a constant in European history.

The Roman Iron Age period was when the conflict in Scandinavia reached its peak. Chiefs and rulers constantly competed for fertile land and followers, who would become their military force. Those who were in power remained so because they had the means to defend themselves and conquer others. During the Iron Age, the Scandinavians started building their first defensive constructions, such as walls, ramparts, bridges, and roads. Although it is difficult to determine their age, some ring fortifications in Sweden are believed to have originated from the Late Iron Age, although they were similar to the ring forts of the later Viking Age. Nevertheless, during the Iron Age, the Scandinavians started constructing hill forts, which were fortified large settlements that rested on the top of a hill. Even some smaller villages were fortified or at least raised in an easily defensible position.

The practice of sacrificing weapons to the gods was still prevalent during the Iron Age, and many of them were placed in sacred bogs, which proved to be excellent for the preservation of items. This is why we now have exemplary evidence and fairly accurate knowledge of the military equipment of Iron Age Scandinavia. The weapons and armor were intentionally broken or burned before they were placed into the sacred bogs with the remains of sacrificial animals (cattle and horses). Human remains were rarely placed in bogs as a sacrifice. It is unclear whether this was done on purpose or if the individuals simply happened to die there.

The practice of sacrificing items to the sacred bogs was distinct to the Germanic people, who rose in Scandinavia during the Bronze Age and spoke the Proto-Germanic language. During the Iron Age, they developed the Proto-Norse language, which would become Old Norse in the Viking Age and eventually divide into the many Scandinavian languages that exist today. Also, during the Iron Age, the first Germanic tribes that would later inhabit continental Europe started migrating southward and occupying the territories between the Elbe and Danube Rivers. By the 4th century, they would establish their kingdoms in the territory of the Roman Empire.

All the weapons sacrificed in the sacred bogs belonged to the destroyed enemies. The lack of human bodies that would typically accompany weapon sacrifices means that the enemy warriors were killed elsewhere or taken as prisoners. Among the sacrifices were boats that were either completely sunk into nearby lakes and rivers or hauled to the bogs in pieces. The weapons came in all possible forms and included battle-axes, single and double blade swords, spears, shields, arrows, and sometimes even armor. They were all bent, broken, or burned so that they could no longer be used against those who captured them in the first place. The most interesting find among the sacred bog hoards was a completely preserved piece of mail armor that consisted of twenty-three thousand metal rings and several scabbards that were lined with fur on the inside. It is believed that this fur was oiled and served as a means of weapon preservation.

The Iron Age in the North and the Sámi People

In Norway, the Iron Age societies were mainly farmers, and they occupied the territories from the south up to Trondheim. They were well connected to southern Sweden and Denmark. Although there were smaller farms on the western shores of northern Norway up to the Tromsø area, these never had the same connection to the developing southern societies as central Norway. Nevertheless, iron deposits existed in the north, and the people extracted them, though in much smaller quantities. They even produced items made of iron, as suggested by the existence of furnaces, and several prominent centers were developed, such as Borg in northern Norway. These farming/iron production societies traded with southern Scandinavia, but it is unclear if they ever traded directly with the rest of Europe.

The farming societies of northern Norway continued to develop more or less the same as during the Bronze Age. The settlements concentrated around the biggest farm, which belonged to the chieftain. However, there is one innovation in the Iron Age settlements of northern Norway that is hard to explain. The large central farm consisted of several buildings for human and animal housing, a longboat, and a central courtyard made out of side-by-side foundations that formed the shape of a horseshoe. No evidence explains what the purpose of these courtyards was. Perhaps barracks were built there, or maybe they were maintenance buildings for the chieftain's farms. But the lack of building material in these courtyards suggests that they were left as open spaces. Some scholars believe these were the spots in which a *thing* would occur. The Scandinavian *thing* was a gathering of people who held legislative and judicial authority. The courtyard might have been assembly places, but more research is needed to fully understand them.

Just like in southern Scandinavia, the northern regions also had local rulers. On the west coast of Norway, inside the Arctic Circle, there is an archipelago with spectacular natural beauty named Lofoten. The evidence of humans inhabiting the Lofoten Islands spans to at least eleven thousand years ago. In the Iron Age, the archipelago was home to a society that didn't mind the complete darkness from December to January, as the sun never rises on Lofoten during this period. Despite the lack of sun, the archipelago has very mild winters. The Atlantic Ocean currents keep the climate temperate, and the sea rarely freezes there. This made the Lofoten Islands the perfect spot for the development of fishing societies, as access to the water was always open. Lofoten was one of the biggest stockfish producers and exporters until very recently.

The waters around the Borg regions were especially filled with fish, mainly cod. This was due to the winter migratory routes. In this region, archaeologists made a stunning discovery concerning the Iron Age settlement of the northern region of Norway. At Borg, the longest Viking longhouse was discovered. In total, it was 83 meters (272 feet), but further excavations proved that this longhouse was much older and that the Viking rulers only expanded it. Originally, the longhouse was 67 meters (220 feet) long, and it was built during

the 5th century CE. It had four rooms and two entrances, one on each side of the longhouse. Later rulers added one more room and created five separate entrances. The longhouse was built completely out of wood, and although it was destroyed in the 9th century, archaeologists managed to reconstruct it and build a replica in the vicinity. This site is now the Lofotr Viking Museum; it's open to visitors and hosts an annual Viking-themed festival.

Aside from the longhouse, the Borg excavation site was rich in various items dating from the Iron Age. Among these items were sickles, scythes, various hooks, racks for drying fish, many tools made of iron, arrowheads, and four swords. There were also many items made of gold and glass, which testifies that Lofoten had a good connection with the rest of Scandinavia and was open for trade, maybe even warfare. The discovery of high-status gold-foil figures indicates that the Borg rulers were rich, respected, and of importance to the region and period.

The inland areas of northern Scandinavia remained populated by hunter-gatherer societies, which were believed to be the ancestors of the Sámi people. The Sámi people are indigenous to northern Norway, Sweden, Finland, and the Russian Kola Peninsula. They are known for preserving the semi-nomadic lifestyle of reindeer herders, though, in modern times, most of them are well integrated into the rest of the Scandinavian societies. Only around 10 percent of the Sámi are devoted to reindeer herding. Although reindeer herding is a traditional way of life for the Sámi people, it appeared relatively late, in around 1500 CE.

In the 19th century, Scandinavian historians believed the Sámi people occupied only the northernmost territories. However, new evidence disproved this theory, and it is now a consensus that the Sámi used to live anywhere between central Norway, Sweden, Finland, the Kola Peninsula, and the far north. It is also believed that the Sámi had been present in Scandinavia since the Stone Age, but they only began developing their social and ethnic identity during the

first part of the 1st millennium CE. In prehistory, the societies of Scandinavia were pretty homogenous, but in time and due to contact with the societies of southern Scandinavia and continental Europe, some groups of the population started developing unique cultures and identities.

Although it is not known when the Sámi people formed their separate identities, it is obvious that they were a distinctive group during the Scandinavian Iron Age. They lived parallel to the farming societies of the western coast of northern Norway and occupied the inland regions, where they were free to hunt and lead nomadic and egalitarian lives. (Unlike the farming societies, the Sámi never had class divisions.) The Sámi and the Scandinavians had a symbiotic relationship that was based on marriages, gifts, and trade. It is believed that the Sámi of the interior first introduced falcons, walrus ivory, and fine fur to the south. The farmers of northern Scandinavia may have acted as the middlemen between the southerners and the Sámi, and they collected taxes on the Sámi trade. The Sámi also became very dependent on the products from the southern Scandinavians, especially iron tools.

The archaeological and historical evidence suggests that the relationship between the Sámi and other Nordic groups of people was based on respect and cooperation rather than on violence and oppression. However, in more recent years, the Sámi people were oppressed and discriminated against. These major problems came about when the governments of Scandinavian countries wanted to assert sovereignty over the northern lands. They forced Scandinavization and Christian baptisms on the Sámi. They wanted to forcefully integrate the indigenous people, and they banned the Sámi languages and culture.

Chapter 3 – The Viking Age in Norway

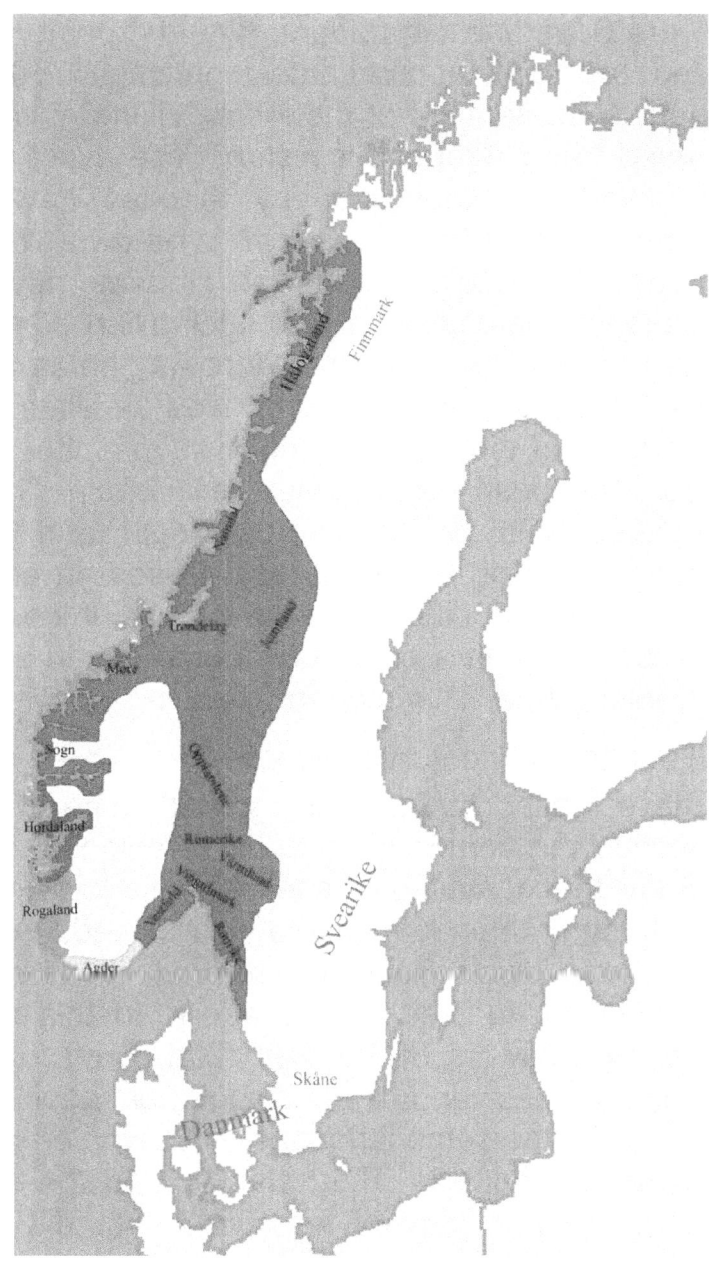

Norwegian petty kingdoms, circa 872.
https://commons.wikimedia.org/wiki/File:Norwegian_petty_kingdoms_ca._872.png

The Vikings were Scandinavian raiders, farmers, poets, and singers who dominated the seas approximately between 750 and 1066. However, the modern meaning of the word "Viking" is very different from what it used to be throughout history. The exact origin of the word is still unknown, although many theories have been put forward. But the meaning of the term is known. When it first appeared in the Old English language, it was never used to designate a nation or belonging to a Scandinavian ethnicity. It was simply used to describe the foreign raiders as pirates. In the Latin translation, the Old English word "wicing" was translated to "pirata." The first appearance of the word "Viking" was in written evidence in Old English, but that doesn't mean that was its origin. The word may have a Proto-Germanic or Old Norse origin and a meaning somehow related to sailing and nautical activities. In any case, the term Viking today has a different meaning, as it designates the Scandinavians who lived in a certain historical period that we often refer to as the Viking Age. This modern meaning was invented (and romanticized) during 19th-century nationalism.

The Vikings never called themselves by that name. They lived in communities occupying certain geographical regions. They referred to each other by the names of these regions; for example, they would call each other men of Jutland, Hordaland, Vestfold, and many others. They didn't have a national identity, and they expressed loyalty only to their local leaders. In this regard, they named each other followers of Thorkell, Olaf, Cnut, or Svein. But they did form alliances and fought together against common enemies. They spoke the same language—Old Norse—and enjoyed the same culture and religion. They also shared the runic writing system, fashion, art, and way of life. Only later did a sense of national identity develop. They started calling themselves by their national names, such as Danes or Norse. In the medieval period, the Danes were all Scandinavians of the southern regions, while the Norse were those who inhabited the northern regions.

Not all Scandinavians were Vikings—only those who indulged in raiding and pirating. The majority of Scandinavians remained farmers and craftsmen; only the minority were practicing "Vikings" Modern scholars prefer to use the term Vikings just for the raiders and Scandinavians for the rest of the people who inhabited the peninsula. Sometimes they even like to separate the northerners and call them Norse simply to make the differences between them and the inhabitants of the southern regions of Scandinavia.

The term "Viking Age" refers to the end of the Iron Age and the beginning of the medieval period, but the term itself was coined in the 19th century to make the periodization of excavated items in the Copenhagen Museum easier. Since then, the term's meaning was expanded, and the public started using it to designate a period of very much romanticized barbarians of the past. With this new meaning, the "Viking Age" entered popular culture and expanded outside the borders of Scandinavia.

During the Viking Age, Norway was defined as a geographic entity for the first time. It became obvious that the people who inhabited the Norwegian territories saw themselves as a separate community from the rest of Scandinavia, and they started developing an independent identity. They had separate rulers, kings, and chieftains who would ally themselves with the Danes and Swedes in their efforts to colonize the new lands. But conflicts between different Scandinavian groups weren't uncommon either. At this point, Norway begins to differentiate itself as one nation. However, through alliances and constant contact with other Scandinavians, Norway remained bound to the history of the whole peninsula. Norway's connection to neighboring states would remain visible until the 20th century.

The Viking Age in Norway

Until recently, it was thought that the Viking Age started with the first recorded raid on the abbey of Lindisfarne, England, in 793.

However, later excavations proved the presence of early English and Irish items in the graves of Norwegian chieftains of the early 8th century. This means that the first contact was established much earlier than originally thought. There were many significant social and cultural changes in Scandinavia that occurred during the late 7th and early 8th centuries that led to the first overseas voyages and early contact between the Vikings and the Brits and Celts. The most important was the development of much larger ships capable of sailing in the open waters of the vast seas and oceans. Previously, the Scandinavians sailed in much smaller canoes that were able to safely navigate the shallow coastal waters.

The modern countries of Scandinavia didn't exist during the Viking Age, but the clear separation between the communities existed. Most of Europe and the British Isles had already accepted Christianity and formed kingdoms that more or less resembled the modern states. But this wasn't the case in Scandinavia. During the early Viking Age, the Scandinavians remained pagans and maintained their tribal divisions, with many chieftains forming the aristocracy of the Scandinavian society in general. But this changed by the 10th century. Many Viking leaders sailed to Europe, where they adopted not only the new faith (Christianity) but also new ideas of governance. When they returned to their homeland, they tried to implement these new ideas. By the 12th century, Christianity had been largely adopted, and the royal authority and kingship were set in place. The Viking leaders were no longer simply chieftains but kings that ruled by laws, edicts, and various privileges. By the 13th century, each Scandinavian country became a nation-state in its own right.

During the early Viking Age, Norway was composed of several petty kingdoms and earldoms. They were of different sizes, with the smallest ones comprising only several villages and the biggest one occupying the territory of several modern counties. Little is known about this period since written sources didn't exist. Almost everything we know comes from archaeological discoveries, and the many kings and earls of Norway are mythological and legendary figures, which means their actual existence is questionable. Nevertheless, the territory occupied by all these small kingdoms and earldoms was already referred to as a single geographical entity.

One of the Norwegian chieftains of the 9th century, Ottar fra Hålogaland (English: Ohthere of Hålogaland), visited the king of Britain, Alfred the Great (r. 871–899), and told him stories of his travels. His account was documented in *Seven Books of History Against the Pagans* by a Roman priest named Paulus Orosius. Ottar talked about his homeland, which was, according to him, situated in the northernmost of all Norse lands. It is believed that his kingdom, which he called Hålogaland, occupied the territories of the southern Troms og Finnmark district between Namdalen Valley and Lyngen Fjord. But Ottar talked about his kingdom as part of the land of Norsemen, which he called *Norðweg*, or "Northern Way" (Norway). The chieftain also spoke of *Dena Mearc* (Denmark) and *Sweoland* (Sweden), clearly making a difference between the three Scandinavian nations. He even mentions the Sámi people naming them the *Finnas*, but he also gave an account of *Cwenas* and *Boormas*, who also spoke the Sámi language and are considered different tribes of the Sámi people.

Ottar continued his traveling stories and described Norway as a long and narrow country. He also claimed that north of Hålogaland, there were no permanent settlements until one sailed to the southern shores of the White Sea in what is today Russia. It is through Ottar's account that the Norwegians and Norway entered history as a separate, individual country with very distinct people. Ottar considered himself a leader of his people and equal to the Anglo-Saxon king. But his farmstead had no more than ten cows, twenty pigs, and some arable land. Nevertheless, he was considered a wealthy man in Norway, and most of his wealth came from hunting, trading, and taxing the Sámi people.

At this point in history, the Norwegians shared the same language, culture, and religion with the rest of the Scandinavians. But they considered themselves a separate people, and it is possible that they were seen as such by their neighbors. They were separated by natural boundaries. Thick forests and mountains in the east divided Norway from Sweden. In the south, the Danes had their domain, which was separated from Norway by the lay of the land. It is possible that due to this obvious separation, the Norwegians started developing their own cultural and ethnic identity.

The farm continued to be the main unit of land and source of livelihood. However, Norway's geography is such that, even today, with all the modern technology available, only 3 percent of the land is arable. Mountains rise from the western shores of Norway and expand across the country to enter Sweden. The population was confined in the small ledges and plains in the fjords, where they didn't have much land that would produce food. It is believed that the lack of land that could be turned into farms was one of the reasons for the Viking expansion, especially when the population started rising. It was also the reason the Norwegians turned to the sea and started sailing farther away.

The difficult terrain of Norway also made the land routes impossible to traverse. This is yet another reason why the Norwegians turned to sailing. One of their goals was to establish sea communication routes, and naturally, they turned to the west. The first Vikings who approached the British Isles were probably the traders from Hålogaland, but it didn't take long for these traders to turn to raiding. They were also the first settlers in the western and northern islands, such as Greenland, Iceland, and the Faroe Islands. From these islands, in the year 1000, the Norsemen sailed farther west to the coast of North America. They landed in the area of Newfoundland

(*Vinland*). However, they never managed to establish permanent settlements there.

The Vikings' expansion wasn't limited only to the west. They entered continental Europe and reached the shores of the Mediterranean. The Vikings even served in the armies of the Byzantine Empire and were influenced by Christianity. They also crossed the Baltics and traversed Russian territory, sailing the rivers to the Black and Caspian Seas. But these were mostly the works of the Danish and Swedish Vikings, as the Norwegians concentrated their efforts to the west and sometimes to the east, where they would sail to the White Sea. No matter where they settled, the Scandinavians had a lasting impact on the area, and they even organized little kingdoms within these new territories. In Ireland, they founded Dublin, and in England, the Norse kings ruled in York. They quickly adopted the more sophisticated forms of rulership that were already in place in medieval Europe, and they realized the significance of the urban centers. The Scandinavians brought the idea of these cities back to their home country.

The Unification of Norway

While Ottar fra Hålogaland was giving his account to the Anglo-Saxon king, Alfred the Great, Norway was going through political changes. The last three decades of the 9th century saw the settlement of Iceland, and during this time, the famous Battle of Hafrsfjord took place. The battle was well documented by the Norse skaldic poets and chroniclers, but its exact date is lost. It is believed it took place anywhere between 872 and 900. The Viking chieftain Harald Halvdansson (later known as Harald Fairhair) won the battle and started the process of unifying Norway. In reality, this battle brought Rogaland and Agder under Harald's control and nothing else. But in the popular imagination of Norwegians, this battle was the key moment of the unification of the whole country.

Modern scholars believe that the unification of Norway came as a result of a century of internal political changes. Nevertheless, the result was the same as the popular belief about the Battle of Hafrsfjord. Harald Fairhair emerged as the sole ruler of the vast territories of Norway, and he started ruling as Harald I. The

Heimskringla (sagas about the Norse kings) of 13th-century Icelandic chronicler Snorri Sturluson describes how Harald conquered all the Norwegian petty kingdoms one after the other and how the Battle of Hafrsfjord was just the conclusion of this unification.

The geographical nature of Norway made it very difficult for the early kings to assert power over their neighbors. The most powerful ones who managed to conquer more territories had to sail their ships up and down the rugged coast of Norway to collect products from the farmstead that owed them their allegiance. This was the only way the Norwegian leaders could assert their power, and it was very unlikely they were able to control vast areas at once. But there is no reason for scholars to doubt the story of Harald Halvdansson and his unification of Norway. However, it's very unlikely he ruled Norway alone. With the level of political organization and the instruments of power exercised in Scandinavia during the Viking Age, it is more likely that Harald ruled through alliances with other petty chieftains.

Even though Harald didn't unite Norway under his direct rule, he started the process of unification, which his successors would follow. But Norway's unification wasn't a unique case in Scandinavia. At approximately the same time, Denmark and Sweden underwent the same process. These developments in Scandinavia had a strong influence on the rest of Europe. The expansions and raids made the European rulers consolidate their power and borders. But by doing so, they provided the Scandinavians with lessons of political organization, and the Scandinavian countries started imitating the European kingdoms.

The three Scandinavian kingdoms, now fully organized, started asserting their dominance on each other, and the wars between neighbors started. Alliances were forged and broken, depending on the political trends, which changed often. Norway would help

Denmark against Sweden just to suffer Danish and Swedish attacks a year later. The Scandinavian kings also competed for the control of the same territory since they all had territorial ambitions in what is today Norway and Sweden. The Danish kings were the strongest during the Viking Age, and through their wars and their control over southern parts of Sweden and Norway, they asserted their dominance on the whole peninsula and had a deep political influence on it.

The Territorial Consolidation of Norway and the Viking Kings

The unification of Norway fell apart after the death of Harald Fairhair in 930. The sagas mention that Harald allowed his eldest and favorite son Eric (later known as Eric Bloodaxe) to rule alongside him. Eric inherited the throne of Norway after his father's death and defeated the armies of his brothers who wanted to partition the kingdom. However, Eric proved to be a despotic ruler, and he lost the support of the Norwegian nobility. At this time, his younger brother, Haakon, who was fostered at the court of the Anglo-Saxon King Æthelstan (r. 924–939), returned to Norway. The nobility was more than eager to replace Eric and raise his younger brother to the throne. With the help of Sigurd, Jarl of Lade, young Haakon took over Norway. Eric Bloodaxe was forced to flee to Orkney, but his sons remained and fought for their right to rule. The country was yet again partitioned, and a conflict for dominance started, which would last until the 11th century.

This conflict between the Norwegian throne pretenders was just the first phase of the territorial consolidation of Norway. Some jarls were more successful than others, but the permanent success of uniting the country once again eluded them all. It was hard for Eric Bloodaxe to assert his dominance over the land, as he was known to travel, which means he was away from his kingdom for extended periods. According to the sagas, Eric started raiding when he was twelve years old, and he sailed to Denmark, the Baltic, Germany, France, Ireland, Wales, Scotland, and later to Lappland and

Bjarmaland. Some Norwegian sources even claim he entered what is today Perm Krai (Principality of Great Perm) in Russia. He is thought to be the same person as Eric, King of Northumbria, but this is often disputed by modern historians since there are no reliable contemporary sources that confirm this claim.

Eric's youngest brother Haakon was nicknamed "the Good" and "Adelsteinfostre" (foster son of Æthelstan). He spent most of his life outside of Norway since he was sent to the Anglo-Saxons at a young age; his father wanted to protect him from his dangerous, power-hungry brothers. This might have been the reason he had trouble keeping Norway unified. Although he had the support of the nobles, as he promised them the abolition of the inheritance tax imposed by his father, not all wanted to follow a foreigner. He had to defend his right to rule against Eric's sons on different occasions. In 953, he fought a battle at Avaldsnes in today's Rogaland county. He proved he was superior to Eric's sons by winning the battle and killing Guttorm Ericson (one of Eric's sons). The next battle against his enemies was in 955, and Haakon again emerged victorious. This time, he killed another son of Eric, Gamle. In 957, the sons of Eric attacked again; this time, they had the support of the Danish king. Haakon once again defeated them.

But he had to pay a high price for the final victory over Eric's sons. In 961, at the Battle of Fitjar, Haakon was mortally wounded. After his death, he was succeeded by Eric's eldest surviving son, who ruled as Harald II and was nicknamed "Greycloak." However, Harald II couldn't persuade all the Norwegians jarls to follow him, and he exercised his power only over western Norway. He was killed in 970 by a fellow Norwegian jarl named Haakon Sigurdsson, who at the time was allied with the famous Danish king Harald Bluetooth.

Haakon became the *de facto* ruler of Norway, and he ruled as a vassal of Denmark, though he managed to preserve Norway's independence. He was firmly against Christianity, which was slowly penetrating the country, as Haakon the Good had tried to convert

Norway. Haakon Sigurdsson ruled approximately between 975 to 995. He was a popular ruler at first, as the people liked that he was against Christianity. However, he was a notorious rapist, and he would persuade many noblemen to send him their daughters under the pretense of marriage. He would rape them and send them back to their fathers. These actions made him very unpopular with other jarls and petty kings across Scandinavia. He lost their support just as his enemy and throne pretender Olaf Tryggvason rose to power.

According to the sagas, Haakon was killed by his slave, who hoped to get a reward for his deed from Olaf. Once he became king, Olaf punished the slave for betraying his master and had his head put on a spike next to Haakon. Olaf I was the great-grandson of Harald Fairhair, and he is one of the most important individuals in the history of Christianity in Norway. Legend has it that Olaf I built the first church in Norway, but he used violence to persuade the people to convert. He was the founder of the Norwegian city of Trondheim, which was his seat of power.

The story of Olaf's downfall is a very interesting one, though its historical accuracy cannot be confirmed. The sagas tell a tale of Sigrid, a Swedish widow queen who was proposed to by Olaf of Norway. However, Olaf demanded she convert to Christianity, which she refused. In a rage, Olaf hit Sigrid with his armed glove in front of all of her followers. The Swedish queen was so infuriated that she started gathering all of Olaf's enemies to bring about his downfall. She united the armies of Sweden, Denmark, and Wendland (Pomerania in today's Germany), and the united army fought Olaf at the Battle of Svolder in the Baltic Sea. This is considered the largest naval Viking battle, and it took place in the year 1000. Olaf had only eleven ships, and he faced down seventy enemy ships; he had no chance of winning this battle. Instead, he decided to throw himself in the sea. What happened to him is unknown, but he was presumed dead. Norway was ruled by the jarls who were loyal vassals to the kings of Denmark and Sweden.

The last Viking king of Norway was Harald Hardrada (r. 1046–1066), also known as Harald III. His predecessor, Magnus I, became the king of Norway after the death of Danish King Cnut the Great. Several years later, he also claimed the crown of Denmark and ruled it until his death in 1047. As his successor, Harald Hardrada claimed the crowns of Denmark and England but was unsuccessful in keeping them. He was the half-brother of Olaf II (later canonized and known as St. Olaf), father of Magnus I. The Danish King Cnut exiled Harald to Kievan Rus, where he served as the military captain of Grand Prince Yaroslav the Wise. This allowed him to gain military experience and later serve as the commander of the Varangian Guard of the Byzantine Empire. When he finally came back to Norway in 1046, his nephew, Magnus I, accepted him as a co-ruler. They ruled together for one year before Magnus died.

Harald's reign was famous for its peace and prosperity, as he established his coin, the first one in the history of Norway, and a foreign trade network that would serve Norway during the Middle Ages. But to achieve sole rule after the death of Magnus, Harald had to fight off jarls who tried to claim the throne. He was successful, and he outlined the Norwegian territorial unification under a single government. He founded the city of Oslo and made it his capital. Harald died in England, where he had gone to claim the throne, in the famous Battle of Stamford Bridge, which ended the Viking Age. The second stage of Norwegian territorial consolidation would occur during the Scandinavian medieval period.

Old Religion and the Spread of Christianity

Like other Scandinavians, Norwegians followed the Old Norse religion. Unlike Christianity, this Old Norse religion was a system of beliefs and rituals, and it had many variations depending on the region in which it was practiced. The Norse gods were not as divine as the Christian God, and they lived and behaved as humans do. They lived on farms, married, and had children. They warred against each other or other supernatural beings, and they acted out in rage and fell in love with each other. Norse gods were even mortal, and one of them, Baldur, died. Norse mythology has very developed myths and stories about the ancient gods, and most modern people have heard at least some of them, as they have been popularized in pop culture (for example, Thor, Odin, and Loki). These gods accepted sacrifices from humans, and the gods would help them in return.

Interestingly, the practitioners of the Old Norse religion didn't have a concept of religion. To them, the gods, rituals, and magic were integral parts of life, just as their farms, wars, and families were. The concept of religion was introduced only with Christianity. This is what allowed the Old Norse religion to accumulate different variations, as it was never canonized, and the people who practiced it were free to do it in their own ways. Different communities had different rituals that had the same goal. Marriage rituals might have been different in Sweden than in Norway, and different gods could be invoked during the ceremony, but the result would still be a marriage between two people.

Aside from the gods, the Norse revered many different supernatural beings. The most widespread ones were the Norns, the female figures who shaped the individual and collective faith of humans. Scandinavians also recognized the powerful beings named *jötnar*, who were the ancestors of the gods but also their main enemies. There were different types of *jötnar*, but many academic texts simplify the variety of supernatural beings and simply designate them all as giants (though they were not necessarily that large). The giants were not evil by nature, as some of them, such as Skadi, belonged to the pantheon of gods. The Norse also believed in the existence of elves, dwarfs, guardian spirits, Valkyries, ghosts, and much more.

The Old Norse religion was one of animism and magic. The solutions for everyday problems were found in magic talismans, charms, and magical rituals. Runes were a script, but they were also magical. Each had a different meaning and purpose. Some protected against diseases, while others protected against natural disasters. Odin was connected to magic the most. He sacrificed himself by hanging to achieve wisdom and learn the magic of the runes. Another deity connected to magic was Freya. Her power was feminine magic called *seiðr*, and only several male supernatural beings were able to wield this power. The only male god able to cast *seiðr* was Odin.

The Sámi people had different beliefs than the Norwegians. Their religion was one of shamanism. Because the Sámi people lived in vast areas in the northernmost territories of Europe, their religion and rituals also had variations, depending on their geographical origin. The Sámi religion is closely related to nature, and an emphasis is always put on one's personal spirituality. Each tribe had a shaman who would perform religious ceremonies and rituals, unlike the Scandinavians, who had no concept of priests or religious leaders. The connection between the Sámi and Norse religions cannot be denied, though, and the Sámi are the last people in the world to revere Thor as a god. Most Sámi practiced their old religion

until the 18th century when Christian missionaries were sent to convert them.

Christianity first appeared in Norway in the 8th century, but it didn't take hold. The raiding Norsemen would bring home Christian stories, ideas, and relics, but they were seen only as curiosities. The first king who tried to introduce the new religion to the country was Haakon the Good. He was brought up as a Christian in the court of Anglo-Saxon King Æthelstan. He even brought monks from England to spread Christianity in Norway, but the pagan jarls rebelled against the new religion and killed the missionaries. Some stories claim that these pagan jarls even forced Haakon to apostatize.

Other Viking chieftains and rulers also accepted baptism, but their main motivation was to strengthen their ties to foreign rulers. The attempts at conversion were also used as a political play, as the newly Christian kings could now replace their political enemies and elevate Christian followers in their place. Harald Greycloak was one of the rulers who were baptized during their visits to foreign countries. He accepted Christianity in Northumbria and tried to introduce it to Norway. However, he was quickly forced into exile and didn't have much time to work on mass conversion. After his reign, Norway came under the control of Danish Christian King Harald Bluetooth. He tried to forcefully convert the region of Oslo but not with much success.

It was believed that King Olaf Haraldsson (St. Olaf; r. 1015–1028) completed the Christianization of Norway. But today, modern scholars understand that Christianization was a process and that the significance of Saint Olaf is more symbolic than real. He was a Viking king, and he fully acted as one. Although he was Christian, his worldview continued to be pagan, especially regarding such themes as war and love. Nevertheless, he did impose Christianity on his subjects and used cruelty to do so. The miracles prescribed to him were later invented so that Norway could have a domestic saint to whom to pray. He even received some attributes of old pagan deities so that the transition to Christianity would be easier for the Scandinavian "heathens." The cult of Saint Olaf served to consolidate Christianity as the national religion, and it gave the Norwegians a foundation for their national identity and unity.

Chapter 4 – Norway in the Middle Ages

Infant king Haakon Haakonsson being taken to safety by the Birkebeinars (19th-century painting by Knud Bergslien).

https://commons.wikimedia.org/wiki/File:Birkebeinerne_ski01.jpg

The last phase of Norway's unification and territorial consolidation was a period of civil wars. Norway lacked political unity, and it was ruled by many kings who once again divided the country. After the death of Sigurd the Crusader, who ruled Norway from 1103 until 1130, his son, Magnus, wished to unify Norway once again. But he was forced to share with Harald Gille, who claimed to be Sigurd's half-brother who was born and grew up in Ireland. They ruled together for four years before Magnus started preparing for war against his co-ruler. Although he initially defeated Harald and forced him into exile in Denmark, he was later captured and blinded, and Harald ruled the whole of Norway alone.

The dispute for the Norwegian throne lasted for the next hundred years, with the Swedish royal family Sverre finally winning exclusive control over the whole country. Their kingdom was known as Birchlegs (Old Norse *Birkibeinar*), named after the political party that opposed the previous Norwegian king, Magnus V. The Birchlegs were so named because it is said they were so poor they couldn't afford pants (or shoes in some sources), and they wore birch tree bark instead. After the death of King Sverre, the Birchlegs fought the Bagler faction, which consisted of the Norwegian aristocracy. The Birchlegs were victorious, and they used it to install Sverre's grandson, Haakon Haakonsson, on the throne of Norway. Haakon's reign marked the end of the civil war and the unification of Norway under a single ruler.

During the rest of the Middle Ages, the Norwegians concentrated their efforts on expanding to the north and east along the coast of Finnmark. Jemtland (Jämtland), which is now part of Sweden, belonged to Norway at this time, although the population was mostly Swedish and belonged to the Swedish church, not Norway's. This resulted in the incomplete integration of Jemtland, which would later bring the loss of this province. To the south, Norway stretched to the mouth of the Göta River, which is also in Sweden today. This was also the point where the three medieval Scandinavian kingdoms met: Norway, Sweden, and Denmark.

The Medieval Church, Aristocracy, and Wide Society

The territorial unification of Norway lasted for so long because it was a process in which it was necessary not only to conquer the land but also to create a national identity that would bind all its people into a unique and singular society. This society had to be independent of the ruler, at least to some extent, so that it could continue being united even after the death of the kings who held it together. All of this was achieved during the 13th century, though significant steps were made much earlier with the first kings of Norway.

The Norwegian aristocracy was a significant factor in uniting the country, mainly the relationship between the jarls and local chieftains with the king. The kings had to bind the aristocracy to themselves to exercise their power in areas that were far away from their capitals. But the chieftains had immediate benefits from being bound to the ruler. In return for their loyalty, they received a portion of the royal income, patronage, and prestige. The kings and chieftains cooperated, but this administration wasn't easy to maintain. The chieftains tended to be loyal only as long as it was beneficial to them. They never felt the need to serve the country as a whole, and there was little to no patriotic drive behind their actions.

Because of this, the monarchy always strived to strengthen its relationship with the aristocracy. To achieve this, the kings would transform the local chieftains into *lendmann* (men of land). This meant that in return for their loyalty and service, the chieftains would receive a portion of royal lands that would be added to the land that was already theirs. The chieftains who refused to become *lendmann* were driven out of Norway or killed. Thus, the early kings secured the territorial unification of the kingdom.

During the Early Middle Ages, the relationship between the Crown and the church was more positive than the one between kings and aristocracy. The kings remained the leaders of the Christianization of the population. But the kings were also the church builders, and they donated the land that would later become ecclesiastical estates. This land was usually confiscated from the peasants who persisted in their pagan faith. The bishops were appointed by the kings, and they often had a place in the king's retinue. Only from the reign of King Olaf Haraldsson (1015–1028 onward did the bishops start to take up a permanent residence. First, they settled in Trondheim and Bergen and later in Oslo.

The Norwegian kings were mostly baptized abroad, and they learned the relationship between the church and the monarchy from other European countries. They wished to bring this relationship to Norway, mostly because they saw how it could be beneficial to the establishment of kingship. Christianity and the church served to break the old pagan society that refused loyalty to a single ruler by constructing a new one under the leadership of the king and the church. In time, the whole country was dotted with local churches. The ecclesiastical network they created across Norway served to bind society into a single countrywide social system.

The kings were the head of the church and its main protector. As such, their power was immense and undeniable. Through the church, the kings were the protectors of society, and their status among the people of Norway was the most exalted and holy. The clergy served the king as counselors and helpers because they were educated. They could also read and write, which was something not all members of the aristocracy were able to do during the Early Middle Ages. The clergy also had connections with the rest of Europe and informed the king of the more advanced social organizations that existed abroad. Through their religious work, they shaped society according to the king's wishes.

The main bulk of the Norwegian medieval society was the peasants. As they represented the majority of the population, it was the peasants' opinion that shaped the political scene of the monarchy. To please them, the kings needed to provide the peasants with a feeling of security and well-being, and they did so through military protection and their ability to uphold the law. Legal and political stability was achieved by pleasing the majority of the population, and in turn, they gave their support to the monarchy.

Some kings were lawmakers, but all of them upheld the laws because it would bring income to the Crown through fines and confiscations. The legal and administrative apparatus had to be built to maintain the law, and a judiciary system was created, which served the kings as yet another power base.

The military protection that the king offered the peasants was based on the mutual help of all involved parties. The king was the military leader, and he guaranteed the safety of the peasants. But it was the peasants who provided the king with ships, weapons, manpower, and food. This led to the creation of a conscripted army, which would become a great naval force. Such a naval force was first organized in Vestlandet during the reign of King Haakon Haraldsson (Haakon the Good), and it later spread to the rest of the country.

The relationship between the peasants and the king had one important feature: the popular assembly known as the *ting*. This assembly has its origins in prehistoric times, where general meetings of the people were organized throughout the country (Alting). The judicial matters and those of common political interests were dealt with during the *tings*. In the Middle Ages, these assemblies were transformed into local bodies, and they operated in both towns and the countryside. Some assemblies were given a special role, for example, the acclamation of the kings, and they had a series of legal ceremonies during which the kings and the peasants exchanged pledges. Because the peasants represented not only the majority of the population but also a very powerful political force, these acclamations were necessary, and all throne claimants sought them.

The Lagting was another form of assembly that formed during the Middle Ages. Unlike the Alting, the Lagting gathered the representatives of various communities that occupied a certain territory. The representatives met to discuss and deal with the things that concerned multiple peasant communities in the area. The Lagting was also the highest judicial assemblies in the kingdom, and they served to ratify the laws. But it was the monarchy that organized the Lagting, and the king's involvement can easily be understood. Through these assemblies, the monarch could legally associate important government initiatives with the people that inhabited large areas of the country. For example, through the Lagting, the monarchs introduced Christianity to the rural areas of the kingdom.

The first towns and cities were formed by the kings in a time when the need for secure administrative and military bases rose. The old estates along the coastal shipping routes were not enough during medieval times because the population grew, and the monarchs also needed to strengthen the kingdom's centralization. But the Crown also wanted to promote and exploit the economic activities that are often associated with the urbanized areas than with the hinterlands. In the Middle Ages, these activities meant trade and crafts. The first established towns were Trondheim, Borg in the Lofoten archipelago, Oslo, and later Bergen. These towns soon became the bastions of royal and ecclesiastical centralization. Soon, the cities became frequently visited by foreign merchants, mainly the Hanseatic League, whose members even started settling in Bergen in the late 13th century.

The Black Death and the Hanseatic League

One of the most disastrous events of the Middle Ages in Europe was the Black Death, an epidemic of the bubonic plague that took anywhere between 30 and 60 percent of Europe's population. The outbreak of the plague lasted from 1347 until 1351, and Norway wasn't spared. In the summer of 1349, the plague reached Bergen. It was introduced by the English seafarers and merchants, and it quickly spread throughout the country. Sweden and Denmark were affected too, but Iceland and Finland managed to avoid the initial pandemic. The Black Death reoccurred in Europe on several occasions until the end of the 14th century.

The population of Norway decreased dramatically during the years of the Black Death, but we do not know the exact numbers. The population decline can only be measured indirectly by observing the societal and economic developments at the time. The farms were abandoned, which was only the first sign of the massive demographic crisis. These farms were a part of the medieval Norwegian economic system, as they produced food and other commodities. Their disappearance meant a steep economic decline.

An economic crisis followed the decrease in the population, and the abandoned farms contributed to the sudden fall in rent prices. But the urban population suffered the fall in rent prices too, as the majority of landowners had a residence in the towns. The rent prices weren't the only ones to drop; taxes and other royal and ecclesiastical revenues were at a loss too. Even the highest layer of society felt the economic crisis. It didn't help that the abandoned farms meant a reduced food supply for the towns, and the urban centers experienced a population decline not only due to the Black Plague but also famine.

The vacuum left by the population crisis, plus the abundance of fish in the Norwegian Sea and timber in the Norwegian lands, attracted investors from abroad, mainly Scotland, the Netherlands, and Germany. They were especially attracted to the towns on the eastern coast of Norway, such as Oslo and Tønsberg. The foreign settlers increased the population of the Oslofjord, where timber activities were very high. The Germans and English were concentrated in Bergen, where the fish industry boomed. The constantly rising prices for dried fish in the world proved motivation enough for many merchants to settle in Norway.

Around 1360, the first Hanseatic trading station (*kontor*) was established in Bergen. The Hanseatic League was a confederation of trading guilds that operated mostly in central and northern Europe, and it was founded in the 12th century. During the second half of the 14th century, the league bought warehouses on the docs (Bryggen) so that their traders could take up residence there. Bryggen is today the main attraction of the city of Bergen, with its many colorful wooden houses dotting the city docks. However, the old medieval houses were destroyed in a fire in 1702; the new ones that were built during the 18th century are still standing. These houses became a UNESCO World Heritage Site in 1979. Most of the medieval settlers in Bergen were German, and they became some of the city's most prominent crafters.

During the Late Middle Ages, the Hanseatic League spread from Bergen and founded offices in Oslo and Tønsberg. While Bergen's *kontor* was controlled by the city of Lübeck, the other Norwegian branches of the league were controlled by Rostock. Both of these cities are today in northern Germany.

The Hanseatic League created a special credit system in Bergen by which they bought the exclusive supply of fish from the northern peasant fishermen. The independent traders that resided in Bergen could not compete with the Hanseatic League, and they came to play a less important role in the city's history. However, the monarchy issued decrees that were intended to protect the Norwegian merchants. These decrees made the natives sole executors of the retail trade.

The Hanseatic Germans tended to keep to themselves and form closed societies within the Norwegian towns in which they settled. However, they only had a completely separated part of the city in Bergen. They strived to isolate themselves, and they even brought about the law in which marriage with Norwegian women was forbidden. They regularly avoided using Norwegian courts when solving the disputes they had with Norwegian citizens. Their presence in Bergen was so strong that they felt courageous enough to defy the Norwegian authorities. They even imposed serious economic sanctions against their Norwegian competitors. The violence between the native and the German merchants and crafters was a common sight.

Norwegian historians regard the Hanseatic League as a negative influence on Norway's economy, as it prevented the development of the native middle class, and its members constantly exploited the northern fishermen. But they often disregard the fact that the Hanseatic League opened a larger European market to Norwegian products, such as timber and fish, which only served to expand the economy of medieval Norway. The coastal towns bloomed because of this new market that the league had opened. There is no denying that a large part of the trade surplus was drained out of the country, but the Norwegian urban centers developed because of the Hanseatic influence.

Toward the Scandinavian Union

During the Late Middle Ages, the history of Norway once again became a part of the wider history of Scandinavia. Through marriage alliances, the royal families of the three kingdoms—Norway, Sweden, and Denmark—became so intertwined that the succession rights led to the unification of the kingdoms under one crown. It all started with the death of Danish King Valdemar IV in 1375. This was the first time in the medieval history of the kingdom that the male royal line was completely extinguished. The Danish throne was inherited by the Norwegian prince, Olaf II. He was the son of King Haakon VI of Norway, who was married to the daughter of Valdemar, Margaret (later known as Margaret I, Queen of Denmark, Norway, and Sweden).

Olaf was only five years old when his grandfather died, and he became the king of Denmark. Because the law considered a ruler underaged until he turned fifteen, Olaf's mother acted as his regent. But even when the king reached the appropriate age to rule by himself, Margaret continued to rule through him. When King Haakon of Norway died in 1380, Olaf became the king of both Denmark and Norway, and he brought the two crowns together. These countries would remain united for the next four hundred years. Olaf died when he was only seventeen, and Margaret became regent of the united countries. While in Oslo, she was crowned regent for life; the Danish kingdom proclaimed she would be a regent until she chose a new king. In 1388, she concluded an alliance with the Swedish aristocracy who had risen against their king, Albrecht Mecklenburg (Albert; r. 1364–1389). The Danish queen regent sent troops to Sweden and defeated Albrecht in the Battle of Åsle Albrecht. But the war continued after Albrecht's death, and Margaret failed to gain control of Stockholm. Finally, in 1395, she managed to take the Swedish capital and prohibit Albrecht from claiming the Swedish throne. In 1397, the Kalmar Union was formed through which the three Scandinavian kingdoms became one.

The Kalmar Union was a completely Danish project, and even today, it is seen in a negative light in Sweden and Norway. Denmark was militarily and economically the strongest Scandinavian kingdom, and it always strove to conquer its neighbors. But Margaret didn't keep the throne for herself. Instead, she chose the son of her sister's daughter, Eric of Pomerania, as the ruler of the Kalmar Union, though Margaret remained the *de facto* ruler of the union until she died in 1412.

In 1434, a rebellion broke out in Sweden after the king refused to acknowledge the complaints of the Swedish of the Dalarna region against their Danish bailiff. The rest of Sweden quickly offered their support to their compatriots, even the aristocracy. In 1439, they deposed King Eric. Denmark also deposed Eric in 1439 but for different reasons. The Danish aristocracy was against Bogislav IX of Pomerania, who Eric chose as the successor of the Kalmar Union. Norway continued to be loyal to Eric until 1442 when the aristocracy decided to follow the example of Sweden and Denmark. Christopher of Bavaria was chosen as the next ruler of the union, though he met a sudden death in 1448.

It is important to understand that the Kalmar Union was never a complete unification. Each country was legally a sovereign state with its own government. This is why the rulers were crowned separately in each country at different points in time. The Kalmar Union also wasn't continuous. There were several short breaks between 1397 and 1523, but in general, the domestic and foreign politics of all three Scandinavian kingdoms were controlled by the same crown. After the death of Christopher of Bavaria in 1448, Sweden tried to remain independent and break out of the union. It was ruled by a series of "protectors of the realm," but the Danish kings continuously tried to assert their dominance on Sweden. Finally, in 1520, the Swedes started a liberation war and proclaimed the dissolution of the Kalmar Union in 1523. They even crowned their own king, Gustav Vasa. However, the union was officially dissolved only in 1570 when Frederick II of Denmark and Norway renounced his claim on the Swedish throne. Denmark and Norway remained united after the end of the Kalmar Union.

Chapter 5 – Denmark-Norway, 1536–1814

Coat of Arms of Denmark-Norway.

TRAJAN 117 This W3C-unspecified vector image was created with Inkscape., CC BY-SA 3.0 https://creativecommons.org/licenses/by-sa/3.0 via Wikimedia Commons
https://commons.wikimedia.org/wiki/File:Royal_Arms_of_Denmark_%26_Norway_(1699%E2%80%931819).svg

To prevent the further dissolution of the union, the Danish king and nobility decided to transform Norway into a Danish province. To do this, they had to get rid of the Norwegian national council, the only instrument of national sovereignty the country still had. The integration of Norway into Denmark wasn't only political but also cultural, and the Protestant Reformation gave the monarch new ideological tools to achieve this. The Norwegian council was finally dissolved in 1536, and although King Ferdinand I promised he would not impose Protestantism in Norway, he quickly changed his mind, as he considered religion the one thing that could unite the people of Norway and Denmark, securing the union in the process.

The consequences of the Demark-Norway union can still be seen in language. To this day, Norwegian is heavily influenced by Danish, and the Danish writing system was completely adopted in Norway. But the Norwegians managed to preserve their national identity and finally broke out of the union in 1814. It is amazing how the Norwegians preserved their distinctiveness through the next three hundred years and got rid of the Danish absolutism through a union with Sweden. It is even more astonishing that this sudden transition occurred without any social frictions and institutional disturbances.

Some historians believe that Norway was never completely integrated into Denmark. Instead, Danish absolutism allowed Norway to grow economically, ideologically, and socially. They also believe that the Danish rule made Norway strong enough to finally stand on its own feet after 1814. However, the other side of history must be acknowledged too. The 16th century was one filled with political, social, and cultural developments in Europe, so it is possible that Norway would follow these trends, even without the Danish guiding them. Some even think that the Danish rule was holding Norway back and didn't allow this country to reach its full potential.

The Early Modern Period

While the rest of Europe regards the period between 1500 and 1800 as the early modern period, the Norwegians simply remember it as the Danish times or the "time of the union." However, just like in the rest of Europe, this was the period in which Norway grew both in population and economically, which prepared the ground for the later industrial revolution. The economic growth was directly caused by the labor divisions, better communication and road system, and the growth of trade. But this development wasn't directly caused by the union with Denmark; rather, it was a continuation of the developments from the medieval period.

The growth of trade was due to the new land discoveries of the 16th century. Norway wasn't directly involved in the explorations at this time, even though its people were known for their daring voyages during the Viking era. This time, other European countries, such as Portugal, Spain, France, the Netherlands, and England, took the initiative. They founded their overseas colonies and started trade. But trade in Norway flourished, as the demand for fish, timber, and iron increased, all of which the country had in abundance. In exchange for these, Norway started importing corn and various finished products.

Although trade and the economy flourished, Norway remained on the periphery of Europe and not just geographically. As a supplier of raw materials, the country didn't experience the same development of various industries as central Europe. Norway's development evolved at a much slower pace than in other parts of the continent. This certainly resulted in a form of stagnation. Norway was in no position to start its own production of finished products; therefore, the need for innovation was very low.

The years between 1500 and 1800 were also a period of conflict in Europe. The new land discoveries and economic demands led to rivalry and open wars. Norway, whose government was outside of the country, wasn't able to decide its fate. Denmark now had the perfect opportunity to exploit the Norwegians and use them as workers and soldiers to strengthen its position in Europe. However, being on the periphery of Europe, Norway was never in imminent danger of having a war on its territory. This allowed the population to continue developing at a steady pace. However, that doesn't mean that Scandinavia was spared from conflict. Territorial wars lasted until the 17th century between Norway and Sweden. Norway was only spared a larger European conflict, which was often even fought overseas in the various colonies.

From 1643 until 1645, Denmark-Norway was in the Torstenson War, also known as the Hannibal controversy (after Norwegian Governor-general Hannibal Sehested). This war was very unpopular with the Norwegian public, as the people didn't want to fight Sweden. But Denmark didn't care about Norwegian public sentiment, and it ordered the attack on Sweden from Norwegian Jemtland. The result of the war was the loss of Norwegian territory, as the Swedish Army not only occupied Jemtland but also continued toward Østerdalen. When the peace was finally reached, Denmark-Norway had to cede large parts of the territory to Sweden. Jemtland was completely lost, as well as the parishes of Idre, Särna, and Herjedalen (Härjedalen). The next war that involved Norway was the Charles Gustav War (or the Second Northern War; 1655–1660), which Denmark-Norway joined in 1657. During this conflict, Norway was split into two parts when the Swedish Army conquered Trøndelag, Nordmøre, and Romsdal. But these territories were returned to Denmark-Norway during the final peace settlement, and this is when Norway got its modern land borders. A special treaty was made in 1751 by which the Sámi people were given the right to cross the border between Norway and Sweden undisturbed, but this treaty completely disregarded the fact that the Sámi had to be considered the subjects of either the Danish or Swedish Crown.

Previous Norwegian territories—Iceland, the Faroes, and Greenland—continued to enjoy trade with their motherland. However, when the final dissolution of the Denmark-Norway union occurred in 1814, these island territories remained under Danish control. Norway exited the union much smaller than it was when it entered it in 1536.

Society and the Crofter System

The main source for the early 16th-period demographics is the preserved tax records that survived the time in most areas of Norway. The taxpayers were listed by their names, and it seems that there were around twenty-four thousand taxpayers in the countryside, all of them peasants and farmers, while the towns had registered twelve thousand taxpayers. For each registered taxpayer, approximately six people should be added to count children, wives, and those who were relieved of tax obligations. This would give us a number close to 150,000 people that lived within the modern borders of Norway. Although there are no official records for the medieval period, it is estimated that there were anywhere between 300,000 and 500,000 Norwegians. This meant that since the Middle Ages, the Norwegian population had suffered a steep decline. However, the census performed in 1801 revealed that 880,000 people were living in the country, which is six times more than during the 16th century.

The growth of the urban population was very fast, even faster than in the countryside. At the beginning of the 16th century, 6 to 8 percent of the population lived in urban centers. By the 19th century, this percentage rose to 10. The towns had clear social divisions, with burgesses (town businessmen) and workers. The burgesses always had their businesses in the town, and they mainly focused on trade, shipping, or crafts. They would often join together in guilds so they could regulate recruitment and trade. They also participated in the internal self-government of the towns. Each urban center was allowed a certain amount of autonomy. There was a clear division, even among the burgesses. The merchants represented the elite, while the crafters lived more modestly. The crafters were regarded as having a better standing in society than other workers.

Many of the burgesses were foreign merchants, especially in Bergen, where the Hanseatic League remained in control of foreign trade until the 1750s when it finally passed into Norwegian hands. Most of the citizens of Bergen were Germans, but it is impossible to determine their exact numbers. It is believed that the burgesses represented less than half the population of the towns, but their number certainly varied from one place to another. During the 17th and 18th centuries, most of the foreigners were Danish. They were considered legal citizens, and they were able to take part in local government. Throughout the Denmark-Norway union period, the foreigners were always the elite of the society, while the Norwegians were often part of the lower classes.

Even during the early modern age, the majority of Norway's population were peasants, up to 90 percent. Within the society of peasants, the crofters were the individuals who rented portions of land (crofts) from landowners and farmers. Although the system was in place in Norway since the Late Middle Ages, the population growth during the early modern period changed the system. It seems that during the 16th and 17th centuries, the crofters made up only a small portion of the population. They were usually older people, which meant they came from the ranks of retired farmers. At the beginning of the 18th century, the number of crofters started rising rapidly. New crofters were young people, and there were approximately fifty-five thousand of them against seventy-seven thousand farmers. This means that around 30 percent of the agricultural community of Norway belonged to the crofters. It is presumed that the population growth and the shortage of food supplies of the later years of the Denmark union forced young people into poverty.

There were different types of crofters: those who rented agricultural land and could work it (crofter's holding) and those who rented enough land for a house and a small private garden (crofters without land). Some crofters rented the land by the sea, and they were called "shore sitters." Crofters didn't pay land taxes because they only rented it. The farmers who owned the land paid the taxes. However, they paid rent and had to contribute to the farm as a whole through other means (either production or as a labor force). From the contracts between the crofters and landowners, we can see that the rent was paid either in cash, in a set number of workdays, or even a combination of these two. These contracts lasted for life, or they were signed for a specific number of years. Some could be broken at any time the landowner demanded.

Crofters never had enough land or animals to support their families. They needed alternative ways to earn income, and they did so by working directly for the farmers. They also sought employment in the timber industry, cutting woods and transporting them down the rivers. Similarly, they found work in fisheries, mines, and the transport of goods. Some crofters had their own businesses, such as petty trading and crafting. If they owned vessels, they usually partnered with other fishermen and earned their living on the seas.

The Economy

In the period between the 16th and 18th centuries, agriculture remained the main source of income, as 75 percent of the Norwegian population drew their income from it. Farms were the main economic units, and all the land between the fjord and the fjell (mountain) was considered a farm. The infields were made out of arable land and meadows on which the animals grazed. The arable land was constantly cultivated, and the Norwegians learned to combat soil exhaustion with heavy manuring. In some areas, the farmers preferred to rotate their land and plant crops in the grazing fields while the arable land rested for a year. The farms also included forests, and these were used for timber and firewood. In areas with rich forests, the farmers would cut the wood to sell. The mountainsides were used as pastures, and the people would build little mountain houses, where they would spend the season with their sheep and cattle.

Farms were divided into holdings, and they were occupied by different families. One of the purposes of this farmland division was to give each occupant equal amounts of different land. Even the woods were divided and fenced off. Because of this, the holdings had their land mixed up with the lands of other holdings. The pastures, meadows, and haymaking areas were held in common by all the holdings of one farm, and these were sometimes even shared with other farms. However, the population growth during the union period ended this practice, and the pastures and meadows were divided and bordered.

The Norwegian climate limited cultivation, which is why animal husbandry was of equal value as agriculture. There were almost no areas solely dedicated to the production of grain like in other European countries at the time. Arable land was so sparse that the Norwegians persistently grew grain as far north as Troms, even though the crops usually failed there. But the importance of livestock and their numbers meant that the fields were always well manured and fertile, and they were able to produce year-round. Although arable land was sparse, it was able to produce much more food than the European standard at the time.

The first register of what farms produced and how many animals they housed was created in the 17th century for tax purposes. Due to this register, we can now see what the Norwegians used to produce during the union period and how they divided the land. The usual grains produced were barley and oats or a mixture of two known as *blandkorn*. Potatoes were introduced in the 18th century, but their widespread use culminated only during the 19th century. There were many animal species on the farms, but they were all local varieties. This means they were much smaller than the animals today, which allowed them to survive harsh winters on much less food. However, during the abundant summers, the smaller animals reproduced faster.

Fish was always abundant in the Norwegian Sea, especially cod and herring. However, these fish are not easy to extract, especially with the technology of the early modern period. The fish could only be extracted during the spawning season, which lasts for three months. This is when cod and herring come close to the Norwegian shore. However, their spawn is unstable, and people had no means to predict where exactly the fish would go. The fishing business was very difficult, though lucrative. The fishing population couldn't survive only on fish, as their caloric needs wouldn't be met. Therefore, they had to exchange fish for other food supplies. To do this, they had to preserve the fish. Otherwise, it would spoil in a matter of days. Luckily, with the coming of the Hanseatic League, the Norwegian fishermen gained access to the whole European continent.

Land Ownership

Norwegian historian Halvard Bjørkvik estimated the land ownership at the end of the Middle Ages. He claimed that the Crown owned 7.5 percent of the land, the aristocracy 13 percent, the various private hands had 32 percent in their hands, and the largest part, 47.5 percent, belonged to the church. During the period of the Denmark-Norway union, only one land ownership survey was conducted in 1661 by the office of the Land Commission. The significant change in the amount of land owned by different parties is evident. The Crown now owned 31 percent, the church 21 percent, the aristocracy 8 percent, and the private hands had most of the land, owning 40 percent.

The increase of Crown lands is easily explainable. After the Reformation, the king confiscated the church lands, mainly from bishoprics and monasteries. Only the land owned by parishes remained the property of the church. The king claimed these too, though ineffectively. The decline of the amount of land owned by the aristocracy is explained by the decline of the aristocracy itself and the rise of the commoners. Elite families either died out or simply went bankrupt and were demoted to the ranks of the peasantry.

In both the late medieval period and the period of the union, it remains unknown what percentage of the land belonged to the farmers, peasants, and crofters. Today, scholars estimate that around 19 percent of the land belonged to them for the early modern period. But its distribution varied depending on the region of Norway. In the far north, there were few farms, constituting only a few percent of the arable land. In the southwest, this percentage was much larger since the climate there was more appropriate for farming.

In Norway, the free peasantry was on the rise during the period of the union, but this class of citizens didn't exist in Denmark at all. There was a continuous shortage of cash in Norway, and the king was forced to sell some of his possessions, mostly his public estates. The Crown auctioned off the land in two waves. The first one was in 1660, when most of the confiscated monastic land was sold, and the second was in 1720 (after the Great Northern War), when the private estates were sold. During this period, the Crown also sold off the land belonging to the parishes, and the Norwegian churches became private properties.

Interestingly enough, it wasn't the aristocracy that bought the land from the Crown but burgesses and civil servants (*embedsmann*), as they regarded this land as a good investment. Only a small part of the land from the 1660 sale was bought by peasants. But the first generation of the buyers soon started, and they divided the land they purchased into small lots and sold them directly to the peasants. Perhaps the Crown was inspired by this development and started selling the land again in 1720, only this time the sale was made in small pieces of land so that peasants could afford it. That is how the Norwegian peasantry was transformed into the freeholders. However, it remains unknown why the king didn't allow the aristocracy to buy the land, although some scholars believe this was done so that Norwegian agriculture remained protected from exploitation.

Constitutional Politics

The Denmark-Norway union falls into two parts when it comes to constitutional politics. Up until the middle of the 17th century, the union was an elective monarchy. Once a king died, he would be succeeded by a person specifically elected by the council of nobles. This council would subject the new kings to the conditions laid down in a formal agreement. This agreement gave the council the real power in the monarchy, even if the elected successor was the previous king's eldest son. Only the Danish nobility had the right to sit on the council, and they chose the members. The king had no right to appoint new council members. This type of monarchy would be described as the "monarchy of the nobles."

Though the nobles elected the king, other social groups had the right to take part in the governance of the monarchy. In Denmark, the peasants didn't have this right, but in Norway, they did. After all, they represented the majority of Norway's population. Different social orders, such as the nobles, clergy, citizens, and peasants, were all summoned to pay homage and swear allegiance to the king and his elected successor. The different orders would also meet to discuss political issues, such as the sanctioning of specific taxes. However, only the king had the right to summon such meetings, and once they gathered, they rarely took the initiative. One such meeting of the Danish order set the stage for the coup d'état, in which the monarch finally seized full power.

In 1660, the council of nobles lost their power, and the new constitutional politics changed the union into an absolutist hereditary monarchy. This all happened because the council refused to pay additional taxes when the state entered an economic crisis following the wars of 1657 to 1660 (the Dano-Swedish War). The king used the military to press the nobles into agreeing to make the monarchy hereditary. This made all the agreements the kings ever made with the council disappear. The Law of the Realm wrote a constitution in 1665 by which the king was declared the absolute monarch. However, the constitution limited the king's powers in the sphere of religion. Evangelical Lutheranism was acknowledged as the main religion of the state, and the king had no power to change that.

During the union period, the largest administrative unit in Norway was the county (*len*), and it was under the control of the lord lieutenants, who were all drawn from the ranks of the aristocracy. Nine out of ten lord lieutenants of Norway were Danes. Their primary task was to collect the taxes and customs dues for the monarchy. They also had military duties, such as recruitment, and they supervised the legal system and the church. The lord lieutenants worked for a salary and rewards from the king, all of which were drawn from the Norwegian taxpayers.

Although the lord lieutenants had the counties under their control, all administrative work was performed by their servants or bailiffs (*fogder*), who were all picked from non-aristocratic families. The bailiffs were the ones who went out and collected the taxes and dues, attended prosecutions, and carried out the sentences. The king had direct control over the bailiffs because many governmental issues the public had with the monarchy were dealt with during the meetings of bailiffs and the general public. Over time and due to their relationship with the Crown, the bailiffs were transformed from mere servants of the lord lieutenants to the "His Royal Majesty's Bailiffs." They had to swear an oath directly to the king, and it was the king who could appoint and dismiss them.

After the transformation of the bailiffs, more reforms followed. Each of the reforms was designed to weaken the position and influence of the lord lieutenants. During the first decades of the 17th century, a centralized administrative system was set up in Norway. In the rural areas, there were community assemblies. The peasants acted as jurors, but they needed the help of literate and legally competent magistrates (*sorenskriver*). Soon, these rural magistrates came to dominate the community assemblies. The assemblies in towns were made up of a mayor and the town council. These assemblies served the community, and through them, one could contact the court of appeal and high courts if they needed higher legal institutions. In 1604, King Christian IV published the Norwegian Code, but it was only an extension to the 13th-century Magnus Lagabøte's State Law, also known as *Magnus Lagabøtes landslov*, which was written by King Magnus VI of Norway.

In 1630, the monarchy sharply increased the custom dues, but they also introduced some administrative changes to follow this increase. No longer were the bailiffs responsible for the collection of the dues. Instead, the office of the customs service was founded, and it was under the direct control of the king. Another change in the administration affected the army. Previously, the lord lieutenants were responsible for the recruitment, but the government decided to organize a professional army of Norway. This reform was implemented during the 1640s, and the professional officers, who were mainly from Germany, were hired to train the peasant conscripts.

All of these administrative changes in Norway didn't only limit the influence of the lord lieutenants, but they also firmly linked Norway with the government in Copenhagen. With the introduction of absolutism in 1660, Norway became a kingdom in its own right once again. However, this was only in name. In reality, the country was only a collection of administrative areas that were run by a Danish king from the Danish capital of Copenhagen. However, some of the government departments were now allowed to be exclusively Norwegian: the army, the postal service, and the mining ministry. But even in these areas of government, the Danish Crown preferred to organize them into smaller subdivisions and prevent joint Norwegian administration.

The Norwegian Outlook on the Union

In 1720, the interests in the economic development of Norway were rekindled, and many academically educated Norwegians started considering the natural resources their country had to offer. They created topographical maps of various Norwegian localities, and they described the natural environment and economic conditions of the targeted areas. This work sparked self-awareness in the Norwegian academic circles. The authors of such maps and literary descriptions all agreed that Norway was a rich country with a very energetic and independent race as its inhabitants. The Norwegians started perceiving themselves as different from the Danes. In the 1750s, the Copenhagen government opened a debate about the economic question of the monarchy, and it immediately split into two groups: the Norwegian one and the Danish one. The two countries had different resources, industries, and societies. The Norwegians started recognizing that their country was subjected to Denmark and that the relationship between the two countries was based on the oppression of Norway.

During the 1770s, the first history of Norway was published, and it was written by Gerhard Schøning. His work further inspired the already growing sense of Norwegian pride. He traveled across the country to collect material for his history volumes, which dealt with the Norwegian past, from the early migrations until the year 995. However, this sense of belonging to one distinctive ethnic group never reached the majority of the population, the peasantry. It was a movement strictly reserved for the growing bourgeoisie since they were able to afford academic education. Because the peasantry was unaware of the movement, there can be no talk of nationalization in its true sense. Nationalization typically includes all levels of society, and it also includes culture and language.

But a national movement existed, though maybe a more appropriate term would be Norwegian patriotism, a sense of belonging to a specific geographic and cultural place. But such patriotism presented the union with some controversial political issues. In the second half of the 18th century, the Norwegians started demanding a separate university in their home country. The loudest advocates for this change in education were the *embedsmann*, the Norwegian civil servants educated in Denmark. Their main argument was the cost of education. They had to travel far from their homes since the only close university was in Copenhagen. The second political issue regarded the Norwegian national bank, as the bourgeoisie wanted to conduct their business completely locally.

Censorship in the union was very strict, and the wishes of the Norwegians were seldom heard. Norwegians had to wait a long time for their wishes to be fulfilled. Johann Friedrich Struensee, the minister of the Danish government under King Christian VII of Denmark, lifted the censorship of the press in 1770, and the Norwegian grievances were finally acknowledged by the wider Danish population. The first university in Norway was opened in 1813 in Christiania (now Oslo). At the beginning of 1814, the Bank of Norway came into existence.

Although it is easy to conclude that Norway and Denmark started drifting apart during the last years of the union, the truth is that they had close administrative contact. Even the economic contact between the two increased in scale in the years before the Napoleonic Wars, which reached Denmark in 1807. The beginning

of the 19th century was also a period of increased cultural contact. The Danish government actively worked on equalizing the position of the Danish and Norwegian peasantry through a gigantic agricultural reform, but it never came to be.

Chapter 6 – The Union with Sweden

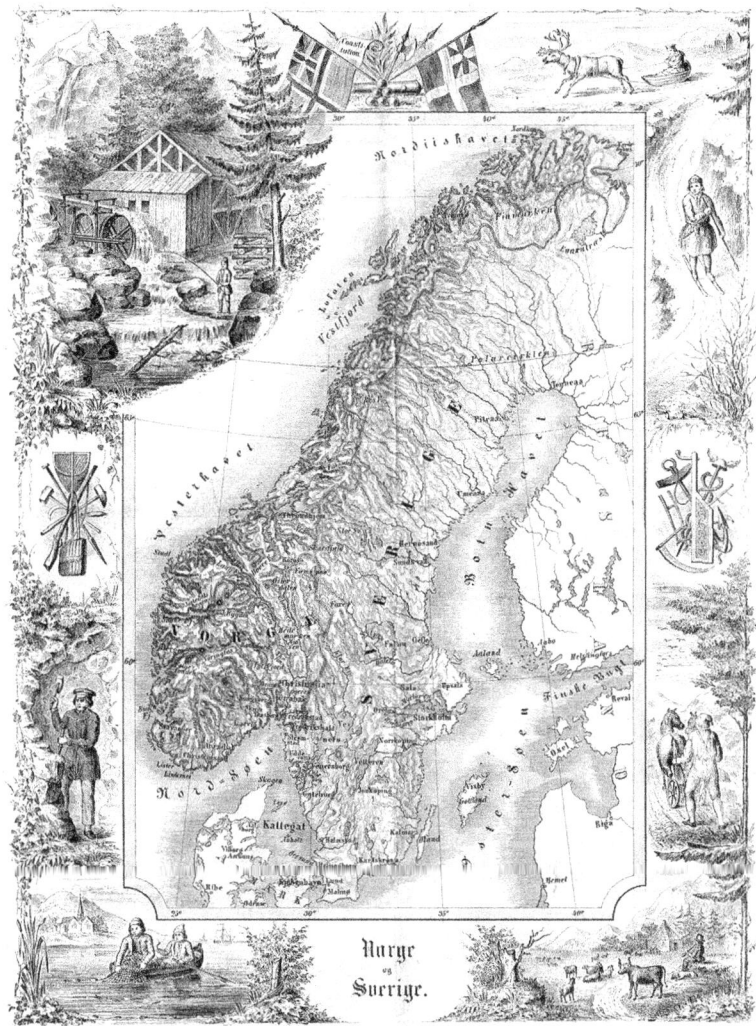

Map of Norway-Sweden from 1847 by Norwegian historian Peter Andreas Munch.
https://commons.wikimedia.org/wiki/File:Norge_og_Sverige_1847_copy.jpg

The dissolution of the Denmark-Norway union came in 1814, but the path to it was much longer. When tracing the events that led to the break-up between the two countries, it becomes evident that it was the international relations and the whole European stage at the time that brought about the dramatic upheaval. The union had a history of foreign affairs being about rivalry and wars, especially with neighboring Sweden. Denmark always strived to dominate Scandinavia, but it could only do so at the expense of its neighbors. Norway had already suffered from being dominated by Denmark, but Sweden wouldn't give up its imperialism dreams.

The Relationship of Denmark-Norway and Sweden

The period between 1536 and 1814 can be split into four phases when it comes to the relationship between the Scandinavian kingdoms. Up until 1625, Denmark-Norway and Sweden had approximately equal military power, and they fought each other for the dominance of not only Scandinavia but also the Baltic and Cap of the North (*Nordkalotten*, the geographical area in the far north of Europe consisting of the Norwegian counties of Troms og Finnmark and Nordland, Swedish Norrbotten, Finnish Lapland, and Russian Murmansk Oblast).

Denmark used the Norwegian forces in its war efforts; thus, Norway got to experience both the Northern Seven Years' War (1563–1570) and the Kalmar War (1611–1613). Both of these wars were fought between Denmark-Norway and Sweden but for different reasons. The Seven Years' War was a product of the dissolution of the Kalmar Union, while the Kalmar War (named so after the city of Kalmar, not the union) was fought to determine who would dominate the Baltic region. During both of these wars, the Danish tactic was to attack Sweden on two fronts. One attack would come from Skåne, which then belonged to Denmark, and the second would be launched from Norway. Sweden would always concentrate on attacking Norway since it was the weaker enemy. But these conflicts didn't solve the domination problem between Denmark and Sweden. The balance of power remained unchanged until 1625.

The turning point came with the Emperor's War (1625–1629). Denmark wanted to intervene in the Thirty Years' War in the Holy Roman Empire. King Christian IV of Denmark aspired to help the

Protestants fleeing the empire, but he also had his interests in the territory of northern Germany. But his meddling in the Thirty Years' War resulted in great military and political losses for Denmark. Instead, the king of Sweden, Gustav II Adolf, won both territories and influence in northern Germany. Sweden gained dominance over the Baltics and became a serious threat to the Danish heartland. They didn't hesitate to take advantage of their new political and territorial position, and in the next two wars—the Hannibal controversy (1643–1645) and the Charles Gustav Wars (1655–1660)—they took Danish territory in what is today southern Sweden and what was once Norway's Bohuslän and Jemtland-Herjedalen, both of which are today in modern Sweden.

In the next two wars, the Scanian War (1675–1679) and the Great Northern War (1700–1721), Sweden took the Danish tactics and attacked from two fronts. However, other European powers got involved in these conflicts, and Sweden had to retreat. In Norway, the defense was organized by the peasantry, just like in the previous wars. However, this time, the peasants weren't enough, and Norway had to create a professional army. Danish and German officers were hired and spread around Norway to enlist and train soldiers from the ranks of the peasantry. Each area consisting of several villages had to provide one soldier. The military effort resulted in Norway being able to provide sixteen thousand soldiers during the Great Northern War.

The Norwegian war efforts became the stuff of legends, as the simple farm boys proved they could put up a serious fight. The Norwegians used these stories to boost their national spirit and mock the Danes, who they saw as acting superior. The Norwegians started feeling proud of their army, which they regarded as a distinctive force separate from the Danish army. As for the naval force of the Denmark-Norway union, it was always based in Copenhagen, but most of its crewmen were recruited from the western coast of Norway. There was no conscription in northern Norway, neither for the land army nor for the naval force.

The Crisis Years

During the American War of Independence and the Revolutionary Wars in France, Denmark-Norway remained neutral so it could strengthen its southern fringes and prepare for a possible attack from continental Europe. The period between 1720 and 1807 was peaceful because Sweden and Russia chose to remain neutral in this conflict. The Norwegian shipping enterprise bloomed because of this neutrality because Great Britain, which was involved in both of these conflicts, lost the markets in its former colonies. However, the Revolutionary Wars turned into the Napoleonic Wars (1803–1815), and with this change, the neutral countries were forced to choose sides. Sweden stood by Great Britain, while Russia chose France. Denmark-Norway didn't have the opportunity to choose. Fearing their great fleet would end up in Napoleon's hands, Great Britain sent its army to besiege Copenhagen in 1807 and forced the kingdom to surrender its navy. Denmark was furious, and its king, Frederick VI, decided to side with Napoleon.

Because Denmark lost its neutrality, its union with Norway became an international point of interest. Denmark chose to side with France, not only because of Britain's act of burning the Danish fleet but also because the kingdom had an age-old fear of being invaded from the south. To prevent this, they chose Napoleon over Britain. However, this choice also plunged Denmark into the conflict against the British allies of Sweden and Russia.

The new wars and the Norwegian involvement in them led to the loss of exports. The presence of the British naval force in Norwegian waters also disrupted the domestic traffic, and most of the links with Denmark were cut off. The Norwegian Army was mobilized, but it waited for further orders at the eastern border. In 1807, the kingdom organized a special committee headed by Crown Prince Christian August to govern Norway during this time of military tension. The prince acted as the commander-in-chief of the Norwegian Army of the south. The first hostilities began in 1808 when the Swedish Army reached the Glomma River. The Norwegians easily defended their position and pushed the enemy back. The Swedish then moved their troops to the Finnish front, where they would fight the Russians. This allowed Norway a brief period of rest. However, the whole country started experiencing famine, especially in 1809. The situation was worst in Østlandet, where an epidemic of dysentery also started spreading throughout the army camps.

But Sweden didn't have much luck on the Finnish front, and the Russian army marched into northern Sweden. The development of these events led to several Swedish officers organizing a coup against their king, Gustav IV Adolf. They put Charles (Carl) XIII in his place. Since the new Swedish king had no children, the Norwegian commander-in-chief, Prince Christian August, was chosen as the heir-apparent to the throne of Sweden. This was done because Sweden aspired to acquire Norway, and Prince Christian was very popular there. They also regarded him as a friend because he refused to attack Sweden while its army was busy on the Finnish front.

By December 1809, Sweden and Denmark-Norway had achieved peace. In 1810, Sweden, Denmark-Norway, and Russia ended the conflict in the north, especially when Sweden decided to abandon its claim over Finland. When Great Britain decided to ease the trade blockade, it seemed that the crisis in Norway was about to end, at least for the time being. But that same year, Christian August, who had changed his name to Carl August, suddenly died of a stroke. Sweden then chose French Marshal Jean Baptiste Bernadotte as the crown prince, who then changed his name to the more appropriate Karl Johan. Although French, Karl (Charles) refused to be Napoleon's puppet and was against a retaliatory war against Russia. In 1812, when Napoleon launched his Russian campaign, Karl Johan abandoned him and sided with Great Britain and Russia, as both of these countries promised Sweden would get Norway for its military help against France.

Sweden long aspired to acquire Norway, but instead, through military conquests, they wanted the Norwegian people to voluntarily agree to the union. Thus, they promised Norway would have equal status with Sweden and would acquire the very liberal Swedish constitution. The Danish government was well aware of the Swedish aspirations toward Norway, and Danish King Frederick VI approached Britain and Russia in an attempt to dissuade them from giving Norway to Sweden. But it was already too late, and once he was declined, Frederick tied Denmark even more closely to Napoleon's France. To keep Norway, Frederick sent his heir, Prince Christian Frederick, to be the commander-in-chief. Christian Frederick and Swedish Karl Johan would be the leading actors in the dramatic events that would soon shape Norway's destiny.

Independence in the Union with Sweden

In 1814, Karl Johan defeated the Danish army just north of the German Duchy of Holstein. He forced Danish King Frederick VI to sign a peace in Kiel on January 14th, in which Norway was ceded to Sweden. Norway thus entered a union with Sweden but as a kingdom of equal status. Christian Frederick received the news of the Peace of Kiel on January 24th, and he decided to proclaim himself as the king of Norway and disturb the Swedish plans. To do so, he needed the loyalty of the Norwegian people, and he planned to visit Trondheim in February, where he would be crowned. However, he was unsure of popular opinion, and instead of immediately taking the crown, he decided to rule as regent until the meeting of the popular assembly that would promulgate a constitution for Norway and elect a king.

Christian Frederick also feared that the Swedes would meddle in this matter. He decided to force the members of the assembly and the representatives of the twelve congregations to swear an oath by which they promised to defend the independence of Norway. To emphasize the seriousness of the oath, they all had to swear in writing. By the end of March, the assembly elections were completed, although the north of Norway did not get involved. The first popular assembly meeting took place on April 10th at Eidsvoll, and the new constitution was drafted by May 17th. Norway was officially restored as an independent kingdom, and a wide spectrum of people gained political rights due to the new liberal constitution.

The Peace of Kiel was thus set aside. But this was only possible because the Swedish Army was busy fighting Napoleon on the European continent. A political vacuum was created between the signing of the Peace of Kiel and the actualization of the Norway-Sweden union, and Christian Frederick took advantage of it. However, this newly created independent Norway had yet to survive the wrath of Sweden.

Karl Johan couldn't let go of Norway, and he wanted to reinforce the agreement made with the Peace of Kiel. He summoned a delegation of the Great European Powers (Great Britain, France, Russia, Italy, the Habsburg Empire, and Germany) to Copenhagen to investigate if Frederick VI had anything to do with the events in Norway. But the delegation cleared the Danish king of any suspicion, and they continued to Oslo. The delegation expressed they felt obliged to accommodate the Peace of Kiel, though they sympathized with Christian Frederick and the Norwegian government he had founded. The conclusion was that the union with Sweden had to be fulfilled, but Norway would receive good conditions in this union.

But Karl Johan was impatient, and he moved his Swedish Army to the border with Norway, demanding the immediate abdication of Christian Frederick. Christian offered his abdication, but he would not allow Sweden to forcefully occupy Norwegian territory as Karl Johan intended. The war between the two neighboring countries began on July 27th, 1814. This conflict was very brief, as the

Norwegian Army stood no chance against the more experienced Swedish troops. The first negotiations took place a month later, and the peace was concluded with the Moss Convention on August 14th. Christian Frederick was forced to hand over Norwegian military fortifications to the Swedish Army. But politically, Christian Frederick won because he forced Karl Johan to accept the creation of a special Norwegian constitutional assembly, the Storting, that would determine the conditions of the union with Sweden. Only after the convocation of Storting would Christian formally abdicate.

The first meeting of the Storting was on October 7th, 1814, and Christian gave up his rights to the Norwegian throne as promised. The assembly then confirmed the Norwegian constitution and revised it to fit the new weaker monarchy and the union with

Sweden. The constitution was ready by November 4th, and Karl Johan was elected as the king of Norway. The Norway-Sweden union would last for the next ninety years.

The Constitution

The most important legacy of the events of 1814 is the Norwegian constitution. It was the foundation of Norway's political life, and the country's basic civil rights rest on it even today. For more than two hundred years of its existence, the constitution went through changes, though the underlying principles and the institutional framework it represents were never changed. It was created by the 112 representatives sent from various communities around Norway, who met at Eidsvoll in Viken county.

In actuality, two constitutions were created in 1814. The first one was on May 17th, and it was intended for an independent Norway. It was based on the principles of popular sovereignty. According to this constitution, the king would have the executive power, while the assembly (Storting) would legislate and determine the taxes. The judicial power would be in the hands of an independent judiciary. This constitution was written for a strong monarchy. It would give the king the power to appoint all *embedsmann* and ministers. The king would also have the power to determine Norway's involvement in wars and peace and make decisions about foreign policy.

The second one was a revision and adaptation of the first constitution, and it was designed for Norway's union with Sweden. It is called the November Constitution, as it was issued on November 4th. The second constitution was based on the same principles as the first one, but it had adjusted the relations between the powers. The king no longer had the power to determine the defense and foreign policies, and the government was given a greater degree of independence. A separate document was issued in 1815 named the Document of the Realm, in which the regulations relating to the actual union and joint institutions were determined. The first lines of the constitution state that Norway is a free and independent, indivisible, and inalienable country, one united with Sweden by the same king. It is clear that although Norway was in yet another union, it had finally received its independence.

Chapter 7 – The New State

A 19th-century mining town of Røros, Norway.
https://commons.wikimedia.org/wiki/File:Kjerkgata_sett_nedenfra_1869_Foto_Elen_Schomragh.jpg

Norway's European borders were finally set in 1826 when a frontier agreement was signed with Russia. During the period between the world wars, Norway would gain territories in the Arctic and Antarctic, its first lands outside of Europe. Christiania became the capital of the country and the center of Norway's political life, but it would not change its name to Oslo until 1925. Since the town had Norway's only university, it also became the center of scientific and cultural life. In 1840, the royal palace and new university were constructed. In 1866, the Storting was built, and in 1898, the national theater was established. Until then, the largest city in Norway was Bergen, but Christiania surpassed it in both population and wealth.

Since the unification with Sweden, Norway started experiencing economic growth as well as a great deal of social change. The population started increasing again and reached 2.2 million in 1900. Today, Norway has around 5.3 million people. Aside from the population increase, the majority of people moved from the countryside to towns. Society and the whole country transformed itself from being the backward fringe of Europe to one of the continent's most developed nations, both economically and culturally. The bulk of the population prospered.

But when Karl Johan was finally crowned in 1818, the whole of Europe assumed an anti-democratic stance, and he thought this was a good time to attack the Norwegian constitution and integrate the country into Sweden's sphere of influence. He planned to cut down the powers of the Storting, which would benefit only the Crown. But first, Karl Johan needed to persuade the parliament to change the written constitution. At first, he chose to do so by force. In the summer of 1821, he gathered the Swedish and Norwegian armies in front of Christiania. However, he changed his mind and decided to take the legislative path instead of the coup d'état.

Karl Johan sent a proposal to the parliament in which he demanded that his power to delay legislation be turned into the power of absolute veto. He also wanted the Crown to have the power to dissolve the Storting and dismiss the *embedsmann*, to have the right to nominate the president of the parliament, and to reduce the Storting's power of impeachment. The king hoped the Swedish population would support his demands regarding Norway and that the Great Powers would at least be sympathetic toward his efforts. But the Swedes thought that if Karl Johan became the absolutist monarch in Norway, he would soon demand the same constitutional changes in Sweden. The Great Powers remained neutral regarding the Norwegian question and opted not to help Karl Johan. After all, they wanted permanent peace in Europe after the Napoleonic Wars. Norway's constitution remained unchanged, and the country got to keep its independence.

Recovery and Growth of Norway

Independent Norway came to be during an economic crisis. The harvest was poor, and the country had low stocks of food. Markets were also closed to Norwegian exports, and the last war drained had all their reserves and provisions. The ensuing inflation meant new problems for the government's finances. However, it took Norway only sixty years to completely recover from this economic disaster,

and at the end of the 19th century, the state had a firmly established financial foundation. Even the population doubled in size due to the better living conditions. However, Norway had to go through a process of growth and recovery to reach the status of a well-off modern country.

The population of Norway exploded during the 19th century, and there are two main reasons for it: the economy and medicine. The agrarian society of Norway improved production, and the increased food import rates brought food surpluses and eliminated famine. Better eating habits also helped the population in Norway to resist various diseases. The survival of infants significantly rose during the

19th century, and the overall life expectancy of the people increased. One of the medical explanations for the increase in the population is the introduction of the obligatory smallpox vaccination in 1810.

The population growth didn't choke the country's economy. Norway managed to avoid the so-called Malthusian trap due to emigration. During the 1850s and 1860s, many Norwegians decided to leave the country in search of religious freedom. They also left because of agricultural failure and the high cost of living. However, the largest movement of the population happened within the country. Many farms in the interior were abandoned, as people moved to the shore where they could enter the fishing or timber industry to sustain themselves or the cities where they could acquire work in the important ports.

After the unification with Sweden, Norway lost Denmark as its biggest market for iron and glass. The industry was hit hard by this loss, especially because British production was its main competitor. But through hard work to overcome these marketing problems, Norway's industry was revived in the 1840s. In just twenty-five years, the demand for new workers jumped, and in 1850, there were twelve thousand people employed in the ironworks. In the 1870s, there were more than forty-five thousand people employed in the same industry. The dominant industrial area was the shipyards. Here, employment jumped from 1,000 to 5,700 people between 1850 and 1870. The sawmills were developed during the 1860s, and by 1868, the new steam-powered sawmills were introduced to Norway. In the timber industry, employment between 1850 and 1870 rose to thirteen thousand. The new Norwegian industries were the textile factories and engineering workshops.

The modernization of the country started, especially when local entrepreneurs saw the possibility of replacing imported goods with domestically produced ones. The Norwegian tariff of 1842 also protected local enterprises, as they got lower rates on raw materials and semi-finished products. Many of the new producers, especially in the textile industry, had previous experience in the trade, so they knew the market well. They had less trouble opening the production lines and offering their products than the completely new entrepreneurs. They were clever businessmen, and instead of building their factories from scratch, they would import all the technology they needed and focus their attention on what they knew best: marketing. The Norwegians also often traveled to Great Britain, where they could learn the production process and all the technical know-how in the sphere of their industry.

Aside from the expansion of the industry from the 1840s onward, Norway also went through changes in the economic framework of the state. The new and modernized institutions helped the state take on new financial initiatives that boosted the country's economy. By doing so, the state reinforced the development of capitalism. The Bank of Norway focused its efforts on the prevention of inflation and the defense of the value of the Norwegian national currency (the Norwegian krone). The state helped the development of industry by taking up foreign loans, especially in times of crisis. In 1851, the Norges Hypotekbank was founded as a state credit institution that drew foreign capital into the country and gave the citizens long-term real estate mortgages. The private commercial banks found Norway a prospective market and started opening their offices around the Norwegian towns.

The government also realized they needed to invest in roads and communication networks. With the opening of new and modernized roads, transport prices dropped, and postal services were extended to include many new areas. Between 1855 and 1870, the state built a national telegraph network, which was immediately linked to the effective international communication system. Because of increased postal needs, the first steamships were introduced to Norway as early as 1826. However, the peak of steamboat use came in 1855, and the state alone owned eleven of them. With the steamboats came modernization and development of harbors across Norway.

But the railway became Norway's most prominent symbol of modernization. The first line was opened in 1854, and it connected Christiania and Eidsvoll. In the next 20 years, the Norwegians constructed 594 kilometers (369 miles) of railroads, with firm plans to build another 1,000 kilometers (621 miles) in the near future. This program was finished by 1883, with the state taking full responsibility for the construction and operation of the lines. No foreign companies were employed. The result of the state's devotion and investment, as well as of industry expansion, was the economic growth and improved standard of living for all the citizens of 19th-century Norway.

The Embedsmann State

The period of Norway's development that took place between 1840 and 1870 was known as the age of the *embedsmann* state. This was a period of great political stability and harmonious cooperation of the Storting and government. However, this harmony was occasionally disturbed by the stirrings of the opposition within the Storting. This opposition was the peasants, whose political body was established in the 1830s. It would become a permanent feature of the 19th-century Norwegian parliament.

The leading parliamentary figure of the 1840s and 1850s was Ole Gabriel Ueland, a son of a farmer. He was one of the greatest leaders of the peasants and one of the first peasants who took up politics. Another peasant leader was Søren Pedersen Jaabæk, who was an active member of parliament from 1845 to 1890. During this period, the peasant opposition in the Storting had a very narrow-minded agenda. They demanded the immediate realization of issues concerning the peasantry and were deeply anti-bureaucratic. One of the main goals of the peasants was to curb the power of the *embedsmann*, but they never sought to take up the leadership themselves.

The *embedsmann* had other opposition in the Storting during the mid-19th century. There were the business owners, craftsmen, and academics who didn't become *embedsmann*. This opposition was organized by a young lawyer named Johan Sverdrup, who would become the prime minister in 1884. This opposition group attempted to ally with the peasants in 1851, and together, they organized a tight opposition within the Storting called "the men of freedom," although they later changed their name to "the reform society." But the efforts of the organized opposition ultimately failed.

The main danger for the parliament came from the Thrane movement, which was active between 1848 and 1851. Named after its leader and founder, Marcus Thrane (1817–1890), the movement represented one of the most remarkable protests in Norwegian history. It was the first popular movement in Norway, numbering over 30,000 members within 414 associations. The movement itself began as a protest organization of the laborers and craft workers in the towns, but it soon spread to crofters and the petty peasantry in the countryside. The Thrane movement was ambiguous in its demands. It wanted the implementation of "one man, one vote," which is very democratic. But it also demanded that the king personally act to protect the interests of the commoners. The movement came as a response to the growing pressure on Norwegian society and the increase of the crofter system due to the population growth.

In 1850, the movement presented a petition to the king and the Storting, demanding the equal status of all people when it came to the law, a universal voting system, the abolition of taxes on essential goods (mainly food), state support for poor farmers, and better education for the commoners. The petition had thirteen thousand signatures, but it didn't achieve anything. Thus, the movement turned to revolutionary ideas, but Thrane stopped this idea from escalating. Nevertheless, he was arrested in 1851 and spent the next eight years in prison. With Thrane absent, the movement ended. He later emigrated to the United States and spent twenty-seven years there. His body was returned to Norway only in 1949, and it was put to rest in an honored grave in Oslo.

The *embedsmann* managed to hold power against all the opposition groups because they took the political initiative. Two shining examples of these initiatives are Anton Martin Schweigaard and Frederik Stang. They were both born in 1808, and they were lawyers and members of a youth intellectual movement in Norway, the *Intelligens*. In the 1830s, this movement developed a program in which the Storting and the government were bound to cooperate and take a proactive role in the modernization and development of the country. Stang was a member of the government (1845–1856) and even its leader from 1861 until 1880. Schweigaard, on the other hand, became a member of the Storting in 1842 and remained in that position until he died in 1870. Due to their positions, the two men had the opportunity to implement programs, especially in the areas of the economy.

The Beginning of Modern Norway

At the end of the 1870s, it seemed that the government and parliament had exhausted the fuel that was feeding the Norwegian economic growth. At the same time, the fishing industry started failing, as the spring herring disappeared from the Norwegian waters. The forests were mostly cut down, and the timber industry couldn't afford to export its produce. Sweden became Norway's timber competitor, as it still had dense forests. All domestic industries started suffering as the government failed to secure their protection against foreign competition. Norway had no other choice but to turn to new products, mainly to mechanization and industrialization. It was the only way Norway could keep up with the modernization that occurred throughout Europe.

Ever since its union with Sweden, Norway had its ups and downs in regards to the economy and development. The parliament's initiatives were a push forward, and they took the country out of the depression that preceded the 1840s. Although the industries, economy, and society grew, it all came to a halt between 1877 and 1887. The growth then resumed, though moderately, and it lasted until the second half of the 1890s. A new depression started in 1900, but it lasted for only five years. Norway started yet another wave of development when World War I happened, making it impossible to maintain the economy. All the various industries Norway developed were suddenly unable to work to their full capacity.

Norwegian modernization was slow, and although it progressed, it was always behind other European countries, especially Norway's immediate neighbors of Sweden and Denmark. But the modernization brought more people from the countryside to the cities, where they found employment in crafts and industry. Although Norway had once consisted mainly of peasants, its demographics had changed. Only a small portion of its population continued to practice agriculture.

The turn of the century saw a dramatic shift in demographics. The people became very mobile, and the cities started counting their population in the millions. While in 1875, only 25 percent of the population lived in towns, by 1900, that number grew to 45 percent. But Norway also lost some of its population during this period, as the emigration to the United States intensified during the 1880s and 1900s. The dominant groups that left the country were young, unmarried men and women, with the majority of them from the rural areas of Norway. In forty-five years, half a million people set sail to America. They did so because of the new labor prospects the United States offered.

Political Changes

After 1884, Norwegian politicians started organizing political parties and recruited for the offices in the Storting and the government. At first, only the Conservative (*Høyre*) and the Liberal (*Venstre*) parties existed. But the two-party system didn't last for long in Norway, and it was quickly replaced by a multi-party one. In 1888, the right-wing oriented members of the Liberal Party separated themselves, and the Moderate Liberal Party emerged. The Norwegian Labour Party was founded as early as 1887, but it didn't win its first seats in parliament until 1903. In 1909, a new splinter party from the Liberals appeared called the *Frisinnede Venstre* (Free-minded Liberals). All the new parties entering the political scene of Norway meant the end of the classic rule by a single party. However, only two of the parties dominated the Norwegian political scene until 1918: the Conservative and the Liberal.

The main point of conflict in Norwegian politics was the union with Sweden, and it remained dominant until 1905. In general, the union was seen as part of the framework of a nation's life, and it didn't pose any massive political questions. However, from time to time, dissatisfaction would rise, and the people expressed their views on the union. Some of their frustrations were over the national symbols, such as the Norwegian flag and coins. Although they took some time, these conflicts were resolved without major disturbances to the population. But some dissatisfactions had a deeper meaning for Norwegian integrity and identity.

One of the issues that Norway had with the union was the fact that the king had the right to appoint a viceroy who would lead the Norwegian government instead of the king. This meant that Norway was a dependent country. In 1859, the Storting annulled the office of the viceroy of Norway, and it was a general belief that the king would approve this decision. However, the Crown backed out of this approval due to the pressure imposed by the Swedish authorities. But in 1860, the Storting made it clear that Sweden had no right to meddle in Norwegian constitutional decisions. The conflict about the viceroy would remain one of the most serious issues that the Norway-Sweden union ever experienced.

Norway had a long history of trying to create a national identity and patriotism. The 1850s and 1860s saw the rise of Scandinavianism, an ideology that claimed that the three Scandinavian countries (Denmark, Sweden, and Norway) were culturally and linguistically very similar. The most prominent advocates of Scandinavianism considered the differences between these three nations to be on a level of regionalism in other European countries. But the political background of this ideology involved the Great Powers, which were posing a threat to the small countries in the north.

Prussia attacked Denmark in 1864, and it wanted it to join the German unification. When that happened, the reality of the Great Powers' threat increased. But the royal line of the Bernadotte family (the Swedish royal house) saw Scandinavianism as a means of uniting all the Scandinavian countries under their rule. However, this was not to be, as Norway declined all the proposals of the Swedish government to tighten the union. One of the Swedish government's proposals was to create a joint cabinet between Norway and Sweden, whose delegates would together make decisions about war and defense. But since Norway refused this, the decision remained completely with the king, his foreign minister, and his cabinet, all of which were Swedish.

Only the Norwegian prime minister, who resided in Stockholm, was allowed a seat in this cabinet, and even then, he was only allowed to attend the meetings that involved Norway. The Foreign Office had two separate bodies: the diplomatic service and the consular service. All the diplomats were Swedish, but the consuls were chosen from the joint cabinet of the Swedish and Norwegian governments, mainly because they had to deal with trade and shipping matters.

But when the Swedish government tried to change the balance in the joint cabinet of the consular service and employ more Swedish consuls, the Norwegians reacted. By doing this, the Swedes would admit they saw Norway as their subordinate. The Norwegian political opinion on the union was now radicalized. During the election campaign of 1891, the Liberal Party promised that, if elected, they would install a Norwegian foreign minister. They won the parliamentary elections, but in light of union politics, they chose to ignore their promise. As an alternative, they demanded a completely Norwegian consular cabinet. The negotiations with the Swedish government about this would last until 1905. The Swedish authorities finally accepted the creation of a separate Norwegian consular service, though it remained under the control of the Swedish Foreign Office.

The Storting decided to establish a separate Norwegian consular service, even though the king had already vetoed it. But the issue was much deeper than that. The Storting interpreted the constitution in such a way that the king could execute his rights only if he had the agreement of his cabinet. Since this was not the case, and since the king didn't form another government that would legitimize his veto, then he was no longer a legitimate ruler. The Storting didn't only establish a separate consular service; on June 7th, 1905, it broke the Norway-Sweden union. According to the Norwegian interpretation of the November Constitution, the king was the only tie between the two countries, and since Norway no longer considered him legitimate, there was no union.

The Norwegian decisions about the end of the union didn't sit well with the outside world. But in the autumn of 1905, Sweden agreed to the dissolution of the union if Norway made certain concessions. The Karlstad negotiations began in August and ended with the Swedish recognition of Norwegian independence on October 26th. King Oscar II renounced his claim on the Norwegian throne, but the Storting offered to elect one of Oscar's younger sons as the king of Norway. But the king refused this offer, and Norway elected Danish Prince Carl as their new monarch. Carl accepted the offer and took the traditional Norwegian royal name Haakon, ruling as Haakon VII (the last Norwegian king with that name was Haakon VI from the 14th century). The Great Powers had nothing to gain with the upkeep of the union, and in 1907, they decided to guarantee Norwegian territorial integrity as an independent state.

Norway Stays Neutral

Norway was independent for nine years before the outbreak of World War I (1914–1918). In those years before the war, the country had to organize its institutions, one of them being the Foreign Office.

Since the Norwegian industry mainly consisted of shipping and the export of fish, and since the country still needed to import great quantities of supplies, the Foreign Office decided early on that Norway should remain a neutral country when it came to alliances. Being on the fringe of Europe, Norway was never of much interest to the Great Powers, and the country didn't want to bind itself to any foreign state that would pull Norway into military conflicts on the continent. The outbreak of the Great War was the first test of Norway's neutrality.

Norway's neutrality was also built on the wish to be left alone so that the country could build itself. The industrialization and modernization of the country were in full swing before the outbreak of the war. Norway was the second country in Europe to introduce female suffrage (after Finland), and it did so in 1913. Besides all the progress that occurred, Norway still had trouble with its food supply, as the number of citizens grew to 2.5 million by 1914. Because of this, Norway had to assume an active international trade policy, and its foreign minister, Jørgen Løvland, believed that Britain was Norway's best trading partner. The Norwegians also believed that if war occurred, Britain would defend Norway.

Norwegian foreign policy was based on their trust in international law and the rights and duties of the neutral countries, which were outlined and drawn up in the Hague Peace Convention (1907) and the London Declaration of 1909. But this trust Norway had in international law was blown to pieces with the outbreak of World War I. Although Norway had no desire to fight in the war and managed to stay out of the conflict, the country couldn't escape feeling the realities of the war. The world was paralyzed, and there was no need for Norway's shipping anymore. The food supplies on which the country was so dependent couldn't be sent to Norway since each country redirected its export surpluses to feed its army. Norway's economy was crushed by the war, even though Norway didn't fight.

As soon as Germany declared war on Russia on August 1st, 1914, all the Scandinavian states issued their declarations of neutrality. But for a newly independent country, this wasn't enough. Norway couldn't afford to be drawn into the conflict, so to reinforce its neutrality, the country issued another declaration of neutrality. To feel safe, the government mobilized the navy and sent Norwegian soldiers to man the coastal fortresses. Thus, the neutrality defense was set in place, even though politically and militarily, Norway was in no position to join the war. The government concentrated all of its efforts on maintaining the supply lines so that the people could be fed and the economy protected. They still remembered how Britain had blocked Norway during the Napoleonic Wars, which resulted in famine.

The people were aware of the consequences a war might have on their country, even if the fighting never reached them. The sale of food products increased, and prices rose dramatically. By August, the banking sector started panicking because the interest rates had started rising uncontrollably. Luckily, by mid-August, the people and banks had calmed down, and the panic was gone. However, the government issued a declaration by which the export of domestic goods was prohibited. Another declaration concerned the price regulations, and more would follow soon after. Norway was also prohibited from selling its ships to other countries. This was done so that the government would have full control over the Norwegian economy.

Norway heavily depended on its merchant fleet because it generated income and hauled the imported supplies. The war at sea caused great distress for Norwegian everyday life. Great Britain

declared the North Sea as a militarized area on November 2nd. By doing this, the neutral Scandinavian countries were forced to oblige Britain's wishes. Norway found itself under British control and thus became a neutral ally. If they declined the British control, they would risk running their ships into minefields in the sea.

A month before the North Sea Declaration, Britain established a new policy of commerce toward Norway to block Germany. On October 15th, 1914, Britain sent a formal letter to the Norwegian prime minister, informing him that Norway had to stop re-exporting supplies that were considered contraband. Norway already had prohibitions on exports, and including the British ones meant its neutrality would be compromised. But Norway also couldn't simply ignore Britain's wishes because Britain kept the Norwegian economy stable. British interference in the shipping of the neutral countries managed to provoke the Germans.

Norway could only hope that the war would end quickly. The prolonged conflict in Europe would demand additional planning, which would only bring new problems to a young government such as Norway. Up until 1916, Norway managed to upkeep its economy, mostly through the workings of Foreign Minister Nils Claus Ihlen, who was a successful businessman. But the foreign minister believed in peace, and he was sure the war would be short. Unfortunately, his ad hoc policies failed due to the prolonged conflict. Germany wanted Norway to remain neutral, as it could keep shipping supplies to Germany if it was. Britain, on the other hand, wanted Norway to join the economic blockade of Germany and deny the enemy much-needed supplies.

By cutting off the export of Norwegian goods to Germany, Norway would lose a great client. It needed to find some kind of compensation, and Britain jumped in, promising to buy all the Norwegian products, mainly fish and copper pyrite, meant for Germany. This was not a great move economically for Britain; the country didn't need that much fish or pyrite since it had full control over American exports too. Norway offered a solution, and soon, the two trade agreements were signed between Britain and Norway. The "Fish Agreement," which was signed in August of 1916, stated that Norway could sell 15 percent of its fish and fish products to Germany, and the rest would be bought by Britain. A similar agreement was made about copper pyrite, in which Norway was allowed to sell only a small portion to Germany. Thus, Britain continued to control Norwegian neutrality, even though by international law, neutral countries were allowed to trade with both warring parties equally.

Norway's business continued to boom during World War I, but only some individuals managed to make a profit. The rest of the population saw an increase in prices and inflation. Nevertheless, there was no need for the introduction of rationing until 1918. The government took certain measures, such as the prohibition of alcohol made from potatoes and grains, the regulation of prices for vital commodities, and an overall prohibition on the selling of alcohol. But the shortages of food and fuel couldn't be avoided, and the black market started operating. This only increased the prices of basic foodstuffs. Even then, Norway refused to introduce rationing, but it finally did so in 1918 after being pushed by the United States. The cost of living rose by 250 percent between the years 1914 and 1918, and Norwegian society was divided into those who could afford the food no matter the cost and those who couldn't. The businessmen who were in the shipping industry got quite rich during the war, and so did the fishermen who sold fish to the Germans on the black market, despite the blockade imposed by Great Britain. Even those who refused to sell to the Germans earned good wages because Britain said it would purchase all Norwegian fish meant for export. But the city dwellers, crafters, clerks, farmers, and labor class starved.

Although the government was financially in ruins, Norway realized it was possible to keep neutrality in times of great wars. But the real reason this was possible wasn't the government's capability to deal with the political, economic, and social difficulties that war brought. It was Norway's geographical position. Since it was on the periphery of Europe, none of the Great Powers had any real interest in this remote country. With Russian and German power reduced after

World War I, Norway had nothing to fear. Its independence was secured, and Norway felt confident that neutrality should remain their defense policy in the future. However, in 1940, they realized that staying neutral was no longer an option.

After World War I, when the Treaty of Versailles was signed, the archipelago of Svalbard was given to Norway. Previously, these islands belonged to no nation, and anyone interested in exploiting the waters around them was free to do so. The whaling industry was flourishing there, and the whaling companies of England, Denmark, Russia, Japan, and Norway took advantage of the rich waters. But once mineral deposits were discovered under the ground of Svalbard, and the mining industry was established there, a government needed to be established that would regulate the laws for everyone living in the archipelago. This honor was given to Norway in 1920, and the administration of Svalbard was established in 1925. The Treaty of Spitsbergen (Svalbard's previous name) made a condition for Norway to allow the citizens of all signatory countries (France, Japan, Italy, Denmark, the Netherlands, the United Kingdom, Sweden, and the United States) to freely settle and start businesses on the island, including whaling and mining. Over time, whaling and mining were replaced by research and tourism industries. Today, the Svalbard archipelago is one of the greatest attractions that Norway has to offer. It is a very remote and desolate place, inhabited by polar bears, arctic foxes, reindeer, and around three thousand people who choose to live there, though many of them leave the archipelago to spend their winter in warmer climates.

Chapter 8 – World War II

The sinking of the German cruiser Blücher in the Oslofjord.
https://commons.wikimedia.org/wiki/File:German_cruiser_Bl%C3%BCcher_sinking.jpg

The years in between the two world wars were difficult for Norway. Small political parties became popular, but it seems that they couldn't keep the government together for long. On average, these small parties would run their term for an average of eighteen months. Norway progressed slowly after the Great War, and it did not amount to much since another war soon broke out in Europe. As planned before, Norway immediately assumed a neutral stance. But this time, the country on Europe's periphery became a significant strategic point, and four of the Great Powers that were involved in the war suddenly needed Norway. These powers were France, Great Britain, Germany, and Russia.

The actions of Russia at the start of World War II proved that Norway was an important territory for the Western powers against Russia. Only three months after the start of the war, Russia invaded

Finland under the excuse that their government was fascist and could become a power base for Germany. But the League of Nations proclaimed this attack illegal, and the fighting ended only three months later, with Russia suffering heavy losses. The Winter War convinced the Western powers of the strategic value of Norway and Russia's military weakness. It also served to convince the Nazi leader, Adolf Hitler, to launch an attack on Russia and to occupy Norway since it would serve Germany's military ambitions at sea.

On April 9th, 1940, Germany started its occupation of Norway. They needed the Norwegian harbors from which they could control the militarized Atlantic Ocean and organize a defense against Great Britain. Norway would also greatly help in transporting the iron ore mined in Sweden back to Germany. The Nazis were aware that the Allies wanted Norway for the same reasons and that their invasion had to be quick. The German invasion of Norway was so well organized and coordinated that even the Western powers admitted it was a daring and unthinkable action. All the ice-free harbors between the Oslofjord and Narvik came under Nazi control early in

the morning of April 9th, and Germany suffered practically no losses. The man behind this very successful occupation was General Nikolaus von Falkenhorst, and in his planning of the invasion, he only used a Norwegian travel guidebook.

To finalize the occupation of Norway, Germany needed to paralyze its political life by capturing the king and the whole government. But the Nazis failed to do this, as their warship *Blücher* sank in the Oslofjord once it engaged in close-range combat against the guns mounted on the Oscarsborg Fortress. This delay gave the king and the government enough time to discuss the situation and decide their actions. The president of the Storting, C. J. Hambro, and King Haakon VII decided Norway should keep fighting the Nazis. The Storting then proceeded to empower the government, creating a constitutional basis for exercising governmental powers under extraordinary circumstances.

Although the government decided to keep fighting against the occupation, they were aware of the hopelessness of it. All the major harbors were already in the hands of the enemy, and most of the arsenals had been lost. The country was already occupied when the mobilization of the army started, and it was painstakingly slow. Even when the soldiers were deemed ready for the front, they had no more than forty-eight days of active training. Because Norway had assumed neutrality would always be an option, the military equipment the country possessed was outdated and in poor shape.

Soon enough, the Allies came to help Norway. Britain responded first and sent troops and military equipment to Norway by the middle of April, with French and Polish troops following behind. Together, the soldiers of Norway, France, Britain, and Poland fought the Germans in the northern regions of the country. Although they were initially repulsed, they took the offensive and freed Narvik on May 28th, 1940. However, they were under constant pressure from the Nazis, and the campaign for Narvik wouldn't end until June 7th. Unfortunately, the Allies had to withdraw their forces to use them in France, and they had to let go of Narvik, which once again came to be the enemy's possession.

When the Allies left Norway, the government had to make a difficult decision. The options were either to completely surrender to the enemy or to continue fighting without the help of the Allies. The government came up with a unique solution. Both of those options were discarded, and it was finally decided to continue the war against Germany but from outside of the country. The king and all the members of his government escaped the country and formed a "government in exile" in London.

Norway Becomes an Ally

Occupied Norway had to break away from its neutrality, and by establishing a government in Britain, King Haakon VII bound his country to the Allies. In 1905, Great Britain offered to guarantee

Norwegian independence, and it was implied that Britain would defend Norway in case of an attack on its territory. This is why Norway sought to bind itself more tightly to Britain, and the Storting had this in mind when they chose the Danish prince for their king, as he was married to a British royal, Maud of Wales, the daughter of Albert Edward, Prince of Wales (later Great Britain's King Edward VII). The Norwegian royal family thus had a strong connection to the British royalty, and it was unlikely Norway would ever willfully join Britain's enemies.

The best asset the Norwegian government in exile had to offer the Allies was its merchant fleet, which managed to stay out of German hands even after the occupation. This fleet made up 18 percent of the world's tanker tonnage. Norway also had the most modern fleet in the world, and since the beginning of the war, it was contracted to the Allied war effort. In April 1940, the government requisitioned its merchant fleet and put it under the management of the Norwegian Shipping and Trade Mission in London. The merchant fleet was the economic foundation on which the government in exile managed to sustain itself. But it was also one of the strongest fleets the Allies possessed in the war against Nazi Germany. As such, it was highly respected and revered. Around three thousand Norwegian sailors lost their lives proving the worth of the merchant fleet. Norwegian soldiers also fought in World War II on the side of the Allies, and they were dispatched around Europe.

Before leaving Norway, the king and the government were sent an ultimatum by the Germans. They demanded the king's abdication and the installment of the leader of the Norwegian fascist party, Vidkun Quisling, as prime minister. At the time, the legitimate government and the king escaped to northern Norway and established the capital in Tromsø. The king proclaimed he would do whatever the Storting decided and that he would offer his abdication if the ministers chose to follow Germany's demands. However, the Storting wanted to continue fighting, and they wanted to defend their king. They refused to legitimately elevate Quisling to the position of prime minister, and because of this, they were forced to flee the country.

Germany finally managed to make Quisling the prime minister. He was the perfect choice because he was willing to cooperate with the Nazis and become the leader of the puppet regime in Norway. Germany then proceeded to prohibit all political parties in Norway except the National Union Party (which was led by Quisling). Hitler appointed Josef Terboven as Reichskommissar, giving him the power to solely appoint all ministers. The "national government" was finally established on February 1st, 1942, by Terboven. Quisling then became the minister president, and the Nazification of the Norwegian society began.

A resistance movement developed in Norway, and it was, in a way, led by the king in exile. Although he had little official contact with the resistance itself, the members of the resistance often wore the king's anagram on their jewelry or clothing as a sign of loyalty to the old regime. Haakon VII became the symbol of the Norwegian resistance movement, and he often used the British BBC worldwide radio network to read proclamations and encouragements to his people suffering under the Nazi regime.

The Country and Society under the Occupation

In the autumn of 1940, the Germans started the Nazification of public institutions and voluntary organizations. There were no more elections for the local councils. Instead, the Nazis appointed individuals who they saw fit. They also tried to get rid of all the clerks and civil servants who were not members of the National Union Party, or at least they tried to force the people to join the party so they could keep their jobs. The bishops and the priests didn't want to suffer this pressure, so they collectively resigned their posts. The teachers who refused to join the regime were deported to the remote parts of northern Norway.

The Nazification of the volunteer organizations proved to be an impossible job. Large sections of the public were involved in these organizations, and it became impossible for the Nazis and the National Union Party members to assert full control over them. The sporting and religious organizations were the first to resist Nazification, and they were soon joined by others. By May of 1941, around forty-three national volunteer organizations protested the Nazification of Norwegian society. The result was the replacement of organizations' legal administration with Nazi ones. The ultimate plan of the National Union Party was to use these replacements to eventually form the "National Council," which would legally replace the Storting.

Living under the Nazi regime wasn't easy for regular citizens. They were forbidden from singing the national anthem or displaying national symbols of any kind. Yet many did so in pure defiance to the occupation. Unfortunately, many people paid for this defiance with their lives. Death was a common punishment, and it was implemented even for simple disobediences, such as listening to enemy radio shows or reading foreign newspapers. Food was sparse, and rationing was implemented everywhere. The urban areas had it much harder than the countryside, as many farmers were able to grow their own food, while city dwellers had to rely on rations. Even toys, books, and furniture were rationed, as well as all imported foodstuffs. Eventually, even locally made bread, butter, milk, and vegetables were rationed.

To get their rations, each family member was given a ticket, also known as a ration book, with which they were given the right to purchase a certain amount of food. To prevent starvation, many people turned to fishing and hunting. Some urban areas were abandoned, with people moving to farms where they could grow potatoes, turnips, cabbages, and carrots. In some towns, the local administration divided parks and green spaces and allotted them to people so they could grow food. Even the flowerbeds between the street lanes were turned into potato patches.

Norway's Resistance Movement

In the beginning, the resistance of Norway was marked by the defiance of the people and the open display of Norwegian royal symbols. But gradually, the resistance started organizing itself into a movement and took military dimensions. In 1942, underground operations began, and by the end of the war, they became one of the main factors of the country's defense. The movement was named *Milorg*, a simple abbreviation of *militær organisasjon* ("military organization"). At first, the resistance only engaged in intelligence activities, both domestic and foreign. *Milorg* contributed significantly to the sea battles between the Allies and the Axis powers. The resistance also helped Norwegian refugees cross the border to neutral Sweden. Sweden alone received some forty thousand Norwegians fleeing the war. The communists in Norway had their own resistance, and throughout 1942 and 1943, they formed a guerilla military organization that specialized in sabotage.

Once *Milorg* engaged actively in the battle against the Nazis, the need for internal organization and leadership rose. They were recognized as the legitimate defense body by the Norwegian government in exile, and an attempt was made to collaborate with the British Special Operations Executive (SOE), a secret organization that coordinated various resistance movements in occupied European countries. But *Milorg* had trouble coordinating things with SOE, which resulted in a series of incidents that caused the loss of civilian lives. The main problem was that *Milorg* became an integral part of the Norwegian High Command in London, which made it answer to British Field Office VI. SOE, on the other hand, worked completely independently and was never able to coordinate events with the Norwegian resistance. SOE finally changed its policy of independence and started working together with *Milorg*. By the end of the war, the resistance gathered forty thousand militarily-ready men. The communist resistance movement remained, operating independently.

However, the Norwegian resistance movement took an active role in the defense of the country only at the end of the war. By then, most of the public institutions were under the Nazis' firm grip, even the police and the press. There was no resistance to Nazification by the local authorities and manufacturing industry. People started voluntarily joining the National Union Party, which gathered around seven thousand members at the start of the war; it had forty thousand members only three years later. Around six thousand Norwegian men joined the German armed forces and contributed to the oppression of their fellow citizens or even went abroad to fight together with the Axis powers.

Norway's civilians were constantly under the pressure of bombing raids. Many cities were continuously bombed by both the Nazis and the British. Narvik, Kristiansund, Molde, Bodø, and Elverum were almost destroyed as early as 1940. Once the Nazis started retreating from northern Norway, they used scorched-earth tactics, leaving Finnmark and Troms devastated. This was considered a national catastrophe, as many people would starve to death. The retreating Germans left only smoke and ash behind them.

After the War

World War II ended Norway's neutrality. The country realized that even though it was on the fringe of the continent, it was an integral part. Its future was deeply connected with the future of Europe. During the post-war years, anti-communist sentiment rose, especially after Russia proposed to share the government of Svalbard. Communism lost all influence in Norway after 1948 when the Communist Party performed a coup d'état in Czechoslovakia. Norway was confident in its neighbors, Denmark and Sweden, even though it had been forced into a union, first with one, then the other country, not that long before. Norway began negotiations with its neighbors to form the Scandinavian defense system. However, these plans were abandoned in 1949 when NATO (North Atlantic Treaty Organization) was formed. Norway decided to become one of its founding members. This meant that Norway was now aligned with the Western powers via a treaty.

Political life went back to normal in 1945, with the Liberal Party continuing its pre-war dominance of the parliament. But the country was devastated by the war and the five-year-long occupation. It needed to focus on reconstruction. Around twenty thousand homes were destroyed by military operations and air raids. In Finnmark and North Troms, all of the buildings were destroyed by the retreating Germans after the Russian invasion of 1944. The production lines and communication networks were neglected during the occupation, and many of them were rendered useless. Many roads and bridges were blown up, and factories were destroyed. This hampered the country's ability to rebuild itself quickly. The influential contemporary economists of Norway estimated in 1945 that the war cost their country some 17.5 billion kroner in its pre-war value.

Norway suffered heavy unemployment before the war, and the situation didn't look much better after it either. With many factories and industries destroyed, the people had nothing to return to after the occupation. It certainly didn't help that inflation was looming, especially because the German occupation took eleven billion kroner from the Bank of Norway during the war. That money was put into the pockets of high officials and never went into circulation to help the economy stand on its feet. But the politicians at the time were aware that no matter what state Norway was in, it had to rebuild itself. The reconstruction work had to begin. The society was eager to work, and it took Norway just one year to reach the output and private consumption of the pre-war period. The manufacturing and fishing industries took two years to recover and reach the pre-war level, while agriculture did so in 1948.

The fear of unemployment proved to be unnecessary. Norway's labor force would rebuild the country, and the economy had to run under its potential. Inflation continued to be a serious threat, but the government held it in check by implementing new rationing policies and employing a strict regulatory system that was kept active until the 1950s.

With the arrival of the 1960s, Norway experienced its first general prosperity after the war. The people were finally able to devote their attention to something other than the reconstruction and rationing of products. During these years, the Norwegians could relax and start focusing on strengthening their ever-growing economy. In politics, the central place was given to the idea of a state based on society and the contribution of that society to the economy. Thus, the idea of Norway as a welfare state was born. Political stability was a major influence on this idea, as all political parties supported the principles of the welfare state. Equality soon became one of the main principles of Norway, which allowed all people to have the same opportunity to secure a good and steady income through their work. Material goods and welfare were equally distributed through society, and the state set up a safety net of social benefits, which would protect the people from poverty due to the loss of income. What made the Norwegian welfare system different from other post-war welfare states was that everyone benefited from it, not only the most endangered groups.

Conclusion

Norway is famous for being one of the most expensive countries in Europe. However, the state didn't reach this status because of its ability to rebuild and develop its economy after World War II. Many European countries could claim an amazing GDP rise and increase in their economy in the years following the war. Although Norway had a unique welfare system implemented, which would help it become one of the most prosperous countries on the continent, it didn't differ much from the rest of Europe at the time. But everything would change during the 1960s with the discovery of oil in the Norwegian waters, away from the shores. When the American Phillips Petroleum Company declared it would start investigating the Norwegian continental shelf in search of oil, the government was quick to issue a decree proclaiming the ocean floor and the underground and underwater areas of the coast under Norwegian sovereignty. This meant that any natural deposits found in these areas could only be exploited by the Norwegian state or through licensing.

In 1965, the Norwegian government issued additional decrees that regulated offshore drilling. Through these decrees, it became clear that Norway wouldn't follow the example of the United States, which distributed allocations through an auctioning system. Instead, Norway followed the British system by which the oil companies had to apply for the allocations. If approved, the government would have financial gains through taxes and royalties after the oil was found. But no oil was yet found, and Norway needed to attract international oil companies to do research. Incredibly low taxes and royalties were set up, especially for foreign companies, as the economy at the time demanded foreign currency. But this doesn't mean Norway discouraged local companies from taking part in the new industry and its development. The biggest Norwegian shipping and industrial companies took part in the early stages of the oil industry.

In 1965, Norway allocated seventy-nine blocks, and almost all of the big international oil companies took part in the research. Only twenty-nine blocks were allocated to the foreign companies that had Norwegian partners. The first drilling started in 1966, and it was the Phillips Petroleum Company that first found oil in the autumn of 1969. The next year, they confirmed that the finding was huge. It contained 534 million Sm3 (standard cubic meters) of oil and 158 billion Sm3 of gas. This discovery was made in the southwestern corner of the Norwegian shelf, and it became obvious that more oil would be found farther north. Realizing this, the Norwegian politicians decided to increase the participation of Norwegian companies in new research and discoveries. In 1971, the Labour Party politicians established a state-owned oil company named Statoil. But this company wasn't fully operational until 1972. After the referendum in which Norwegians decided not to join the European Economic Community (later transformed into the EU or European Union), Statoil started its work.

Statoil would not only bring money to the government. It also served as a regulatory body that determined the pace of oil extraction. It checked the labor and safety standards of the industry and ensured the safety and preservation of the Norwegian environment. But to be able to control and regulate oil extraction, Statoil needed to penetrate all sectors and stages of oil processing. Norway became Europe's largest oil producer in the 1990s and the second-largest exporter. The newly found wealth from oil extraction and processing gave Norway a renewed wind to broaden the social reforms and increase the welfare system. The industry also attracted migrant workers, most of all Pakistanis who came searching for jobs on the oil platforms. The state had enough money to start large investments, such as the National Hospital, Oslo Airport, Gardermoen Line, and many subsea tunnels that connected the country.

In 1994, Norway had yet another referendum, in which it was

decided to turn down membership in the EU. Those who opposed the membership won, taking 52.2 percent of the votes. Even though the Norwegians didn't choose the EU path, the country did join the European Economic Area (EEA), allowing it access to the European international market. The EEA is strictly a commercial treaty and is different from the EU. Later on, Norway joined the Schengen Area, which allowed it to remove border controls and the usage of passports with other member states.

The discovery of oil in the waters of Norway surely propelled the country into the modern era and the 21st century as not just Europe's but also one of the world's most prosperous countries. With its intriguing history and modern ideology of equality, Norway attracts many migrants from all over the world, as well as tourists. Today, Norway is often seen as one of the best countries to live in because of its prosperity, excellent education system that results in extremely high literacy rates, welfare system, low crime rates, and general happiness of its society.

Printed in Great Britain
by Amazon